Nov 12, 1991

For Kaylee Mrochuk,

Thanks for your interest.

All the best to you.

John Lent

The Face In The Garden

The Face In The Garden

John Lent

Thistledown Press

Canadian Cataloguing in Publication Data

Lent, John, 1948-

The face in the garden

ISBN 0-920633-75-7

I. Title.

PS8573.E68F3 1990   C813'.54   C90-097109-6
PR9199.3.L428F3 1990

Book design by A.M. Forrie
Cover illustration by Ann Kipling
Typeset by Thistledown Press Ltd.

Printed and bound in Canada by
Hignell Printing Ltd., Winnipeg

Thistledown Press Ltd.
668 East Place
Saskatoon, Saskatchewan
S7J 2Z5

Acknowledgements

Some of these pieces have appeared separately in the following periodicals or anthologies:
The Antigonish Review, CBC Morningside, The Canadian Forum, Dancing Visions, Event, Prairie Fire, Waves.

I would like to thank the following for their support: Betty Clarke, Allan Forrie, George Larsen, Susan Lent, Greg Simison, Allen Smith and Glen Sorestad. Extra thanks to Peter Greenwood, Jack Schratter, Ria and Marina Von der Ruhr and as always, Jude Clarke. Finally, thanks to the Kalamalka New Writers Society, Ann Kipling, and especially my editor, Paddy O'Rourke.

This book has been published with the assistance of The Canada Council and the Saskatchewan Arts Board.

This book is for my brothers and sisters:
Susan, Harry, Frankie, Mary-Lou,
Michael and Timmy.

◆

CONTENTS

TWO ◆ IN THE GARDENS

THREE ◆ FACING THE GARDENS

EPILOGUE: MUTABILITY

Humility alone designs
Those short but admirable lines
By which, ungirt and unconstrained,
Things greater are in less contained.
Let others vainly strive t'immure
The circle in the quadrature!
These holy mathematics can
In every figure equal man.

—Andrew Marvell,
  "Upon Appleton House"

◆

The very geography of the land and its
climatic peculiarities, the very nature of its
mountains and rivers, the very falling and
lifting of the mists that waver above them, all
lend themselves, to a degree unknown in any
other earthly region, to what might be called
the mythology of escape. This is the secret of
the land.

Other races love and hate, conquer and are
conquered. This race avoids and evades,
pursues and is pursued. Its soul is forever
making a double flight. It flees into a
circuitous Inward. It retreats into a circuitous
Outward.

—John Cowper Powys, *Owen Glendower*

prologue

shelter

Prologue: Shelter

In the end Peter imagined that he could see it.

He could laugh. His father, after all, had taught him to laugh. His father was the funniest person he'd ever met. He still believed his father's laugh and he still lived in it, too. No matter what had happened, no matter what he'd finally seen in their lives, a wonderful, absurd laughter rescued them over and over again. It annointed their blunderings with an arching dignity that could not be diminished. Too real for that. Delicious in its own sheer way.

He could cry. Sometimes, in the end, he did. How could he avoid it? When he peered into all of the self-feeding circles that had enclosed their lives, when he imagined himself as a boy facing those circles, when he imagined his parents or his brothers and sisters as children, he could cry for the puzzling, the lonely and terrible miscues that had whispered to each of those children in the dark. It wasn't a matter of things being undone. He knew that was impossible. He didn't want something undone anyway. He wanted to do something now. That was the hard part, the tricky part. So instead of laughing helplessly sometimes, all he could do was cry.

But there were times when he seemed able to hold both impulses in his head at once: when he saw their lives and realised where beauty grew and what nourished it. When he shuffled into an intersection that faded as fast as he'd stumbled into it. In those moments he knew he'd lurched into the truth of what had happened. And the emotion there was pure. It was a wondering, painful ecstasy. That was his life, their lives, and it grew as richly as it decayed. It was as vibrant under the sun as it was still beneath the snow.

He would try to sing to those moments. After he'd redis-
covered his father out at that cabin on the lake, he promised
himself that he would try to do that. He would let everything
else fall away and hold onto this fragile, green fuse.

1.

That was where it began.

The house Peter grew up in was built in 1948, the year he
was born. It was called a "Golden Home" because it had been
built by the Golden Construction Company as part of the
subdivisions which grew in south Edmonton after the war to
accommodate the baby boom. Theirs was the largest of four
models that this company built thousands of in an ingenious
pattern of concealed repetition. It was two stories high, had
four bedrooms, and was sheathed in speckled brown stucco.
It sported a dark brown shingled roof and trim, and squatted
like an obedient sheepdog on its standard city lot — a sheepdog because it was erratic, constantly moving, wildly flung
in its tolerance of the nine of them living in it. Though there
are always predictable sentiments which cling to the house
you grow up in, for Peter it was specific: the grey room in the
basement sustained him, drew him back.

In 1960, while Peter was being a good senior-sixer in cubs,
playing Little League ball in the spring, and worrying vaguely about when his life would break out of its suffocating
routines, his father was taking the evening news seriously.
He saw himself in an endless series of buoyant Fred MacMur-
ray movies and found himself wanting: he was not doing all
he could for his family. In a feverish clutch of irrational
responses to the hysterias of the time, he became convinced
that their salvation would lie in the installation of a nuclear
fallout shelter in the basement. Secretly at first, then brazenly
as he became more committed, he hired carpenters to attack
the dark grey vacuum of the basement — specifically a
sixteen-foot square to the west of the forced-air furnace.

Peter and his younger brother Richard were outside in the back yard weeding potatoes in the garden, thinking of their time later on down at Scona Pool, when three workmen arrived. It was a very hot Thursday in July; the garden seemed endless. With his shirt sleeves rolled up above his thin elbows, Peter's father talked to these men, spreading out construction plans on the boiling hood of his 1958 Ford stationwagon in the driveway. Peter and Richard tried to overhear the conversation but couldn't catch much except to guess from the odd raised eyebrow and subtle banter among the workmen themselves that they thought Peter's father was a bit of a kook. That was not surprising. His children thought he was a bit of a kook, too. He seemed different from their friends' dads with their workrooms and table-saws and endless photos of fish and deer pinned to the posts in those rooms. But Peter knew his father well enough to know that he was rabid about this project, whatever it was. He had that glint in his eye; he had worked out the details. This would be, Peter found out so much later, his gesture to his children, his gift to protect their futures in the face of the times he'd imagined they'd have to survive. He was also curiously secretive. He gave Peter and Richard money that morning to stay away. This was his territory. They took the money and went swimming.

Within a week, after loads of dirt and clay had been hauled out of the basement on a pulley system rigged through a small window at the side of the house, and after bags of cement had been hoisted down the stairs and piled next to the mixer which had been installed beside the wringer-washer, Peter and Richard stood at the bottom of the stairs surveying the results: three-quarter-inch plywood lay where the basement floor had been. The workmen had dug downward and this was the roof of the project. A well-sealed trap door had been cut into the far corner of the plywood square. This door had been hinged with brand new stainless steel hinges, and had been locked by an enormous combination lock. There was nothing else to see. The workmen had completed their job. They never returned.

Though Peter and Richard badgered him — alternating their stategies between working in the garden for him and whining incessantly — he refused to show them what had been completed down there. And though their mother seemed more sympathetic, almost an ally at times, even she conceded to his secret, rolling her eyes upwards over the dishes, muttering vague things about the money he was spending which could have gone somewhere else.

Throughout that fall their father would descend every Saturday morning with fresh plywood and gyprock and gallons of paint. He had tucked an electrical cord through a tiny hole he'd cut in the trap door, and would lock the door behind him by an inside lock. The odd thing about these new activities was that as far as Peter and Richard knew their father had never done any carpentry before. And though they were drawn like moths to the obscure light of this mystery, too, eventually, in the face of his fierce insistance that they leave him alone, they gave up. In the end they could actually forget that anything unusual was going on down there at all. Other people's fathers worked on rumpus rooms or played golf. In time, they simply saw his time down there as a part of his life, a hobby that pleased him, invigorated him, eased the troubles and tensions he must have endured raising seven children on a teacher's salary in those years.

Somewhere in the midst of all that industry, however, the nature of the times themselves must have altered their father's perception of what he was doing. In the States the hyperactive order and anxiety of the Eisenhower years — the vortex for the kind of hysteria that had grabbed their father in the first place — had given way to other phenomena. A new, buoyant sense of security and culture and sanity had emerged, clinging to the rise of the Kennedy brothers like smoke. And even the national rite of passage which attended their assassinations simply spelled the closure of simple fears and the beginning of more complicated ones. The very notion of a fallout shelter must have seemed mindlessly innocent suddenly. Peter often wondered later how his father must have felt as he accepted that his gift to protect his childrens' futures was having less and less to do with those futures. His children were becoming obsessed by The Beatles, Bob Dylan, by the race riots down in the States, by novels such as *Black Like Me* and *Franny and Zooey*. The one thing that Peter remembered later was his father simply seemed more shy about this obsession that he still nourished. But he still nourished it.

If anything, while Peter, Richard and Evelyn became more absorbed by their new interests in music and in criticising the hilarious innocence of the fifties that had carried them this far, their father became even more consistent in his retreats into the basement. Peter remembered one afternoon in the late sixties when the three of them were downstairs practising for a weekend 'gig' at Giuseppi's Pizza Parlour. They were discussing the sequence of tunes in each of the three sets when their father poked his head in nervously and asked them how it was going. Though he seldom mentioned his childrens' success with the music, they knew he was fascinated by it and even proud of them. He was unlike their friends' fathers in another way now. He didn't seem to get too excited about his childrens' new hairdos and strange music. He seemed quite unsurprised and comfortable with it all. In this sense their father appeared more and more as someone who might have been right about something all along, as someone who had survived the fifties in his own way. That afternoon he admitted quietly to the three of them that he was installing a wood-lathe and some wood-working tools in his room. He confessed that he'd discovered a new interest in hardwoods. "You must think I'm crazy, eh?" he whispered as he glanced sideways suddenly, taking in their guitars and their spangled and beaded denim costumes, then disappeared. They weren't sure what to think.

In 1971 Peter moved down to Toronto hoping to become a folk-singing star and a world-class scholar. These were his dreams. He would return once a year for a speedy visit of hilarious drinking bouts with his brothers and sisters who had stayed in Edmonton. They were very much the scoffers of their pasts then: the social critics of the early seventies confident in their educated and self-indulged privileges and perspectives. Inevitably, Peter would sit with his father over a coffee in the kitchen. They'd crouch over the red aborite table and talk about his teaching. And Peter would always ask him how the work was going downstairs.

"Oh, the usual," his father would say. "Getting things done."

"That's great, Dad," Peter would reply in that lofty, incubated superiority he'd grown into as a hand fits the perfect glove.

"Well, I wouldn't call it *great*, Peter," he replied one time, grinning out the window with a slight trace of sarcasm. "But it will do."

Peter was teaching at the University of Lethbridge in 1975 when Richard phoned him one night in February to tell him that their father had died the night before of a heart attack. Peter was just in the middle of separating from his first wife then, and that, plus other ambiguous defeats that had begun to haunt him, had done their work to deflate the strident confidence he had felt in everything he'd done so far. This news made him wonder even more about the confluence, the odd synchronicity of boundless hope and endless regret.

The funeral was more difficult than any of them could have anticipated. They had each of them loved this man. They were each of them, too, bringing an innocence to this grief, an innocence caused by the mystery he had presented to them. He seemed often to be standing a long way off in a landscape they were unsure of but which he believed in and felt safe in. There was this distance in their father and they puzzled over it trying to breach it.

One morning two days after the funeral, Peter's mother and his sister Evelyn were getting ready to go out shopping at Southgate Mall. It was his mother's first venture out of her grief. Peter was sitting on the bench in the kitchen, crouched over the red arborite nursing a coffee and a hangover. Evelyn was leaning against the doorframe to the left of the stove, waiting. Their mother emerged from her bedroom with a yellowed envelope in her hand.

"He wanted you to have this, Peter," she said to the surface of the table. "I don't know what it is. I never asked him."

After they'd left Peter opened the envelope. In it, folded into a blank sheet of paper, was a key.

Peter phoned Richard to come over right away. He asked him to pick up some rye on the way: that they had something to drink to. About half an hour later Richard pulled up in his half-ton and the two of them descended the dark stairs to the basement with the bottle and the key.

It was not what they had imagined. After the first fumbles for light and their uncertain footing on a set of steep stairs, they discovered themselves in their father's shelter. The lights had been recessed cleverly into the ceiling and shed a soft, clear patina throughout. There was nowhere to sit, so they sat on the floor. The walls, ceiling and floor were smooth, like polished steel, and had been painted in several layers of grey enamel. It was like sitting in a soft, shining grey cube. In one corner there was a small workbench, painted grey, which supported a lathe and three hand vises. Beneath this bench, behind a grey cloth, were stacked a variety of hardwoods and a small box of hand tools. There was something amorphous and unfinished secured in the lathe. To the right of this workbench was a smaller one which held an assortment of paint brushes, steel wool, boxes of sandpaper, and tiny tins of paint and varnish. Richard and Peter leaned back into the wall and passed the bottle back and forth between them. Eventually, Peter got up and climbed the stairs to lock the door from the inside. He returned to his spot and they both sat staring. They were mesmerized by what they saw in the middle of the room.

Here their father had built an eight-foot-square dais which was, like everything else, painted grey. Scattered over its surface lay a number of small glistening red shapes. There must have been about twenty-five of them. Each was different and there seemed no patterns in conventional geometry to describe accurately either each form itself nor the intricate relationship of the whole effect.

Peter stood up and approached the dais. He didn't want to disturb any of these objects, but he wanted to get close enough to examine one of them carefully. It was an elliptical oak sphere which had been stained a deep red, then varnished over and over until it shone perfectly with the deep resonance of ebony. He realised that it must have taken months to have worked this piece into its present elusive form.

Before they could abandon the sanctuary they looked everywhere for clues — a letter, some instructions, sketches, a diary — anything to make this abstraction concrete, this mystery material. Naturally, there was nothing to find. They had entered the soul of a dream and ascended from it that afternoon, up into the stark, flat February skies over the garden, reeling from the rye, but more desperately from their foolish will to reconstitute that soul as he had already done.

2.

This is where it begins. Here.

The house we grow up in is ordinary enough, what is called a "Golden Home," one of thousands built in Edmonton after the war to accommodate the baby boom. My brother Richard and I sleep down here in what our father refers to sarcastically as his masterpiece. It's really a testament to his unflagging inexpertise in carpentry. In some ways, though, it is his masterpiece. You have to know his sense of humor in these matters.

It is a stifling summer afternoon. I am eight; Richard is six. We've been weeding potatoes in the garden for two hours now, trying to please him so he will smile and give us the money we need to go swimming down at the Scona Pool. We are tired of these efforts. Instead, we creep down into the basement to play cards in our room, and we stumble onto him.

He is sitting in the corner of our room on a chair under the window. It is difficult to see him. This cool summer darkness is that thick. With the little light flickering in from the window above his head, this is like staring into the cold world beneath the potatoes out in the garden: so many rich variations and intensities of black. We can only make out that part of his head that bobs into the thin light from the window, and a flashing light that veers off the bottle that is swaying back and forth like a pendulum attached to the blue veins in his right hand. He doesn't seem to notice us yet as we pause, hushed, in the doorway. We hold each other back in our surprise. He is humming to himself. Now his head drops to his chest. All of this happens in a few seconds, but it seems endless to us, seems to happen in some infinitely slow play of light and shadow. He raises the bottle to his lips, gulps some of it down, wheezes, chuckles to himself slowly and begins to cry. Now he is laughing. Richard tugs at my tee-shirt for us to leave. Our father glances up at this soft sound. His head is lurching everywhere in this darkness. I see his face as his eyes catch the light. He is looking at us but he is not focusing. "Is it you?" he pleads, his voice suspended between a surety and a sob. "Is it you, then?"

We scuttle silently upwards in a tortuous slow-motion fear of discovery until now, near the top of these blistered grey stairs, we finally run, lurching, gasping for air, scattering into this violent sunlight of the garden.

one

towards the gardens

varnished red miniatures

The Revenge of the
_____ Landlady's Daughter

Peter left Nelson for Vancouver that summer because he recognised that a part of his life was over. He had always respected the times when a decision evolved slowly, behind his eyes. Though he would sometimes feel that he had been too passive in this process, he also realised that in the crunch he could count on the right decision being made. It was as if he were suspended between the alternatives of chaos and order revolving about him: though one part of him witheld commitments and tested the chaos of inviting time to unfold his purposes for him, another more buried self was judging, assessing and moving itself in an orderly, even precise way. The decision to leave Nelson had been like that; it orchestrated itself in spite of his indifferences as if it were an independent part of him which drew lines and read compasses with care. He knew, too, that he would never return to live in this illusion of Eden and that the only baggage he would carry away with him, as he stuffed the tiny Datsun full of his peripheral worlds, would be the boredom. It was always his enemy in a strange, only partially perceived way, and he was not surprised when it surfaced in Vancouver to stare him down as he attempted to amend his life.

He had opened his briefcase the night before in Princeton in the sleaziest hotel room even he could imagine. It was a warped imitation of an old movie cliche which he thought had been a fiction; he thought they had simply invented such squalor as an effect for the screen. He snapped his briefcase open in this mucus womb to the mickey of rye and the Kurt Vonnegut novel he'd picked up in Grand Forks as prizes for the various pains of his departure. He intended to read and drink his nerves to sleep. As it turned out, even that was hard to do.

His room was suspended precisely above the juke box in the bar below. The music, the pendulous sixty-watt bulb swinging on the end of a frayed cord which disappeared into the green twelve-foot ceiling, Peter himself crouched on the side of the bed in his blue shorts, all of this seemed some black parody of his escape from Nelson. It represented, as an accumulated world, more the reasons for his escape than a new direction. It reminded him of the shape he was in and the kind of world he had been building for himself. It was a world of histrionic laughter, bars, booze, forced smiles and relationships. In the face of that world, this world he sat in now, and the world it sat in, whispered cautiously, "I doubt it." He did fall asleep eventually and dreamed. He dreamed of two women, two worlds, each dancing slightly just perfectly out of his reach. There were keys to both of these worlds and each offered him variations of the greens of paradise, its quiet intensities. He never grasped the keys in those dreams.

When he had arrived in Nelson to teach at the small university there, he had flown out from Toronto and their flat on Brunswick and Bloor. He had confirmed his appointment in a telephone booth on Jarvis Street just across from The Red Lion. He recalled now, in the shredding of his dreams, how in the middle of that call when they were discussing salary, he had glanced up to see the small, hopeful face of Carol outside the booth. Her eyes were brimming with tears and he knew then that she had already accepted that his departure would mean the end of their relationship. He had known this was going to happen for some time now, and he suspected that she knew this more than he did.

They'd been drawn together so young, drawn together by sex and excitement back in Edmonton at a time in both of their lives when each had been possessed by self-confidence. The whole world lay glittering before them, a jewel fitting

itself into the contours of the white gold ring of promise that
defined each of them then. Their relationship had been nur-
tured in an intense, feverish motion that never stilled itself.
And when it did, when they finally slowed down to face the
grey day-to-day ups and downs and bills and boredoms of
their hesitant shuffle into Toronto, they discovered other
rhythms in one another that clashed. Sometimes these
clashes were irrevocable. They revealed too much distance
between them. She felt he was addicted to a panicked speed,
that he would never settle down, become responsible. He felt
that beneath her illusion of non-conformity she was an old-
fashioned girl with rigid, old-fashioned expectations of life
and marriage. He thought she was too desperately ambitious. She suspected he would never follow through on his
ambitions because he was too self-deprecating, too shy to
sieze what he wanted. He felt, at a deeper level, that she was
not a gentle person, that warmth had to be wrestled out of
her violently. She thought he was too friendly, too slavishly
enthusiastic about people. And though they struggled to
deny these differences in the blatant face of them, though
they'd find their real common ground sometimes at night
when their innocent, energized bodies urged one another to
cling to this ecstasy, though they had created a gentle bond
by having disclosed their vulnerabilities to one another,
nothing was as fierce as the differences themselves. Nothing
was stronger. So Peter accepted the job in Nelson knowing
full well that he and Carol were through, that the job would
insure that in time. And he flew off to Nelson with the guilt
he had earned.

   In the midst of that guilt, he arrived in Nelson with what
felt like the beginning of a new life suddenly unfolding
before him. It blossomed in stages, slowly, in the possibilities
of this magical city's turn-of-the-century buildings and the
great, hovering green mountains these buildings had been
carved out of chafing his ears like totems. There seemed an
almost mystical stage of promise here incarnate in the nature
of the geography itself. It had been the fall of 1973 then and

it occurred to Peter that every freak in the country, every counter-culture drop-out in North America had chosen Nelson as the place where his visions would become reality. Waltzing through the ancient granite buildings that clustered together and clung to Baker Street downtown were hundreds of young men and women sporting beards and wonderful long hair, granny-glasses, Indian cotton clothes, clutching guitars, dulcimers and babies in snugglies. They blew into town every Saturday in half-tons and Volkswagen vans from their small properties up in the hills near Kaslo, Ainsworth, Winlaw and Slocan City where they'd built their own cabins and cultivated their gardens. And because the valley was so self-contained, so drawn in upon itself by the sharp pine-covered heaves that created it, these young people were drawn together too, shoved together in a collective experiment: they would try to create a new North-American life-style that cut against the grain of the fifties, that opened things up, that breathed more humanity into things. They'd all meet in the bars and the clubs. They abandoned themselves to the experiment: anything was legitimate; each one of them was unique and valuable; sexuality was open and undefined. And as he began to absorb the intensity of this community, as he began to enter into it in his own slow way, Peter was enthralled by the possibility, the sheer open-endedness of it. He had to admit, too, that he found some of that openness — the loose breasts flashing behind transparent cotton — electrifying, a promise of flesh that grounded the more abstract, ideal possibility. He had never anticipated that there would be so many young people here who shared his own dreams, that he would discover such company in his new life.

Dreams, however, he admitted as the sun fingered the hotel windows like a lover's fingertips, have a way of revealing their hidden textures to you when they are realised. That had happened. Though he could not explain it even to himself, Peter discovered in time that he had leapt into the world of Nelson too eagerly, too thirsty, taking all of its promises too seriously. He had thrown his own innocence into the deep waters there and had surfaced with cynicism instead. He had surfaced mocking his own guilty enthusiasms and irresponsibilities. And he'd discovered that the only thing that allowed him to keep up with the pace of it, the motion of these experiments, was lots of booze. Not for the first time in his life, Peter had to admit that his innocence was being protected behind a wall of abandonment, of sarcastic, drunken motion. He had seen through the experiments to the predictable greed beneath them, and lurched away disappointed and hungover. He didn't know why this always happened to him, but the dream had revealed its hidden textures and the result was a series of trap-doors suspended between the real doors of constant stimulation on the one hand and a horrifying boredom on the other. The self-destruction that issued from his vacillation between these options — his plummetting through these trap-doors — caused his decision to leave, and his materialisation here, in this Princeton hotel room early in the morning, washing his face as if it were his last baptism.

Two days later he stood in front of the Student Housing Board at the University of British Columbia, an overly-earnest version of himself, pen poised for instructions. He was looking for a cheap flat. He tried four on his list with no luck, but got a bite on the fifth. It was a bedroom with a shared kitchen just off 5th and Larch for $75.00 a month. The landlady sounded cautious, suspicious, but resigned. He couldn't explain, even to himself, why he thought that. The house was in Kitsilano, Peter's favorite area in Vancouver. The room was bone-white enamel, had a small single bed, cupboards built into the wall, and a desk under a screened window. It was perfect. It was a soft, white chamber in the heart of Kitsilano. Rohan's Bar with its live rock bands was two minutes away. UBC and its libraries was ten minutes away. There were restaurants and bookstores close by. Peter was excited and anxious during the lengthy interview because he had decided that he wanted this room badly, that it was his hope for sanity.

The landlady was an older but obviously worldly-wise Ethel Mertz in curlers who kept asking him if he was a quiet person. In order to convince her he explained shamelessly that he was a university professor down in Vancouver to work on his dissertation. After this confession she kept repeating the word quiet but for a different audience now. She'd fallen for the doubtful respectability in Peter's disclosure and was now directing and underlining the word quiet for the benefit of the other three tenants who had rooms in this basement and who had each emerged, one by one, quietly, to check out the new arrival. One was a gentle, quiet alcoholic from Nova Scotia. Another was a quiet teenage runaway space-out who had an enormous aquarium in his room. He loved to stare into his fish whenever he was stoned on something which was all the time. The third was a quiet, unassuming East Indian named Sam. He was also working on a thesis, in chemistry. As they all milled around her, nodding, she showed Peter the kitchen, reminding every one of them of its many advantages and of their duties in maintaining those, splicing the word quiet into as many of her sentences as possible. The East Indian smiled wryly and winked at Peter in the midst of her speech. "I've always run a quiet place," she yelled at Peter, "and as long as everybody's quiet and don't bother nobody else, then I run a decent, quiet place." They all nodded enthusiastically, quietly. Peter paid her the rent while the others disappeared. She gossiped a bit about each of them, falling for Peter: him some find, some discovery. "I have a daughter who used to do real good at university," she announced as she lumbered ahead of Peter up the stairs to get her receipt book, flicking cigarette ashes randomly on the carpet. "She knew seven languages. Or was it eight?" The stairs were narrow, steep and low-ceilinged. "Watch your head. There. Lots of people bump into that, ha, ha. Are you OK? Eight languages. That's right. She stays with me now, though. She's been sick." Peter moved

his things into the room five minutes later. It would all begin
here. Quietly.

Since Peter's concern was for discipline, his initial routine
was self-conscious, so much so that it was as if he were
watching himself watching himself. The CBC morning show
would wake him at 7:00 a.m. He'd have a shower, clean the
room from the night before, then head up to the cafeteria in
the SUB at UBC and either plan the day's research or write long
letters, drinking cup after cup of coffee. Or just think and
watch. He'd work in the Special Collections section of the
library, reading Lowry's letters and unpublished material
until the middle of the afternoon. Then he'd drive back to the
flat and go for a run. He went so far as to go into the university
bookstore and buy a pair of running shoes, some gym shorts
and a sweat-top. He watched himself do all these earnest
things. Though his running route varied, it grew eventually
into this circle: he'd run across 4th down to Point Grey Road,
into the listing blue parks, down onto Kitsilano Beach, stop
at the Planetarium for a coffee and a smoke, and then run
back. When he returned he would have another shower,
something to eat, and often fall asleep until 6:30 p.m. listening to the CBC again. In the evening he'd sort through the
Xeroxed material he'd collected on Lowry and read through
critical works concerning the times Lowry had spent in New
York, Hollywood and Mexico in the thirties. Ironies closed
in on Peter swiftly and his circle of enforced discipline was
threatened, even collapsing half of the time.

There were temptations everywhere. They snickered at
the overwhelming boredoms sneaking in on him around
every hour. The boredom was partially a result of his having
contact with no one, and partially of the exhaustion he suffered after his year of teaching and floundering in Nelson.
But the boredom persisted beneath these superficial causes,
however, and he knew it. It involved what his intellectual,
spiritual and physical systems expected from the world:

some stimulation, something to happen, something to laugh at or with: pleasure: movement.

Temptations began to realise themselves in different ways. One day could be warped simply by Peter remaining in the cafeteria instead of going to the library. That's when he'd work feverishly on his own novel. On another day, after hours in the Special Collections — a crypt-like cathedral to sit in not smoking — he'd bolt down Broadway and instead of going for a run, he'd pick up a Thrift Pack of chicken at the Kentucky Fried Chicken near Pine and a bottle of Manor St. David's Claret at the liquor store there. He'd go home, eat the chicken, sleep for a while, then read criticism for as long as the wine would let him. Ironically, he was reading about Hollywood in the thirties, and the fracturing lives of Fitzgerald, Faulkner and Hemingway. He was trying to see answers in their parallel falls which might account more for Lowry's descent. Most of the fracturing here, of course, had been caused by booze and the irony of that didn't escape Peter. He'd often slip out after 8:00 p.m. himself and sit in Rohan's pretending to write in his journal but really listening to Brain Damage, Bruce Miller, Doc Fingers and Blue Williams. He'd get drunk on beer instead of wine as the place went wild with the last spasms of a west-coast looseness imported that summer from the Kootenays, from Nelson in fact. Another temptation was the bar in the basement of SUB right below the cafeteria. Peter rejected that option early on because he'd discovered that this place filled up with exuberant, jockish, fraternity-rich summer students out for the big fuck. Peter found that too depressing to watch anymore. He was living in a different world now. They seemed so stupid in their privilege that they offended something deep in him, some old Nova Scotian ghost perhaps. After a month had passed and he'd gathered an enormous amount of material, another temptation was to take his briefcase down to the Planetarium where he'd work on outlines and drafts of his study of Lowry. He would sit at those tiny white tables the sparrows visited on the deck outside the restaurant and

think: drink coffee, watch the sailboats divide the bay
beneath those pendulous Turner skies.

The quiet in the boarding house turned out to be a hilarious and sometimes dangerous surprise. The three men sharing the basement with him were quiet. They got to know one
another a bit, were friendly, but didn't really attempt to get
close in any way. That was fine with Peter. He didn't want
to get trapped into unnecessary long talks or short fierce
friendships. It was the Tennessee Williams relationship between the landlady and her daughter above him that drove
him out of the house night after night. The daughter was sick
all right: she was an irredeemable alcoholic, a belligerent,
cunning one whose denunciations of mankind, and of her
mother in particular, would begin to build slowly — around
7:00 p.m. if it was a good day — and end in some hysterical
climax — usually thrown objects — around 10:30 p.m. on any
day, good or bad. These climaxes were frequently defused
officially: the police were summoned to the house eight times
while Peter stayed there. Two of these visitations were
caused by the daughter's magnificently ludicrous speeches
to the cowering, conservative neighbourhood around her.
She'd deliver these from the patio deck at the back of the
house where she'd grip the railing uneasily, always some
shred of a Blanche Dubois remembered, half-remembered
dignity. She'd sway in her half-opened fortrel housecoat and
regale the Walt Disney innocence around her with what she
imagined as a variety of existential sarcasm: "Oh sure. *Sure.*
Pretend that everything pleases you. That your paltry life has
unfolded perfectly like some great fucking *rose* for Christ's
sake!"

One night when Peter had forgotten his key, he made the
enormous error of knocking on the landlady's door to see if
she'd let him into his room. He was confronted by the
daughter instead, their first real encounter. Her Scotch-
quilted face was a shifting montage of laughter, tears and
serious, lengthy stares intended to transmit some deeply

understood message between them. She wanted to help Peter out. Yes. But somehow first she had to discover cryptic parallels between his rather simple plight and her more serious one. Being locked out of things was the essential motif. Finally, after heaving a large tin of Empress Strawberry Jam through the sliding glass doors to the patio, unfortunately closed at the time, she was able to flush her mother out of a locked bedroom. She must have barricaded herself in there to save herself from a not-so-uncertainly squalid death at the hands of her own daughter. "You fucking cunt!" the daughter shrieked in triumph as her mother emerged in curlers and fumbled with a gargantuan key ring, "I should kick your ass into your fucking tomorrows!" Peter finally got the key and disappeared. The cops arrived on schedule a half-hour later: some neighbor concerned about murder, such obvious sin. In the morning Peter cut out two sides of the screened window and left it unlatched so that he could avoid that melodrama in the future. It seemed difficult, sometimes, to hang around the place for anything but eating and sleeping. The daughter was a constant threat to him now. She was always lurking upstairs searching desperately for a sufficient audience. She eyed him cunningly through the curtains sensing a sympathetic possibility: an easy mark. One afternoon, driving back to the flat with a slowly cooling Thrift Pack of chicken beside him on the vinyl passenger seat, Peter spotted the daughter and the gentle alcoholic living downstairs with him stumbling home together with a fine bag of booze. He almost wept for this alliance and the possibility that some vague romance might alter the direction of her evening anger.

Peter was obsessed with boredom. He felt that if he could discover a key into its corrosive effect on his energy, he could also discover a route back into the rich kind of solitary health he had known when he was younger. He found his present situation frustrating: here he was, twenty-seven, living in the most beautiful city he'd ever stayed in, doing the work he'd always wanted the privacy and time to do. Instead of

ascending into heights of achievement and smiles, he felt he
was descending into the depths of complex attempts to complete things and maudlin sessions late at night when he'd
simply sit on the edge of the bed and weep, thinking of his
life so far.

The boredom seemed to thrive in a very real space Peter
sensed between contradictory wills waging their wars inside
of him. On the one hand, Peter had always felt driven to work
hard. He loved challenges and loved creating things out of
the energy he gained from confronting those challenges. This
energy seemed endless at times and had turned him into a
student in the truest sense of that word. And he respected
this drive. On the other hand, there was a subversive side to
his spirit that undermined the first, ordered side. This second
self encouraged Peter to suspect his achievements, to apo-
logise for them, to undercut them with a growing gift for
cynicism. This second self existed almost purely in the present tense: it sought out pleasure, wanted gratification immediately. What it wanted was usually physical and in time
concentrated its energies on booze and sex. Because Peter
was such an earnest soul, he juggled these selves meticulously, slavishly aware of their operations, never allowing either
side to emerge completely victorious. In this third, neutral
state, however, boredom grew and multiplied. If he'd been
working too hard, he'd allow himself to let down. If he got
bombed enough he'd feel guilty about that for days and enter
into a slow depression which could only be rescued by a
return to order. If he hadn't been such a serious soul he might
have ignored this war. But that was never easy for him. He
couldn't help himself. And the landlady's daughter's
speeches didn't help much either. He had waged his own
wars long enough to recognise the ridiculous truths she
spoke. It occurred to him that peace lay somewhere in that
third, neutral state where the boredom thrived. He wanted
to solve the mystery in the heart of that territory.

Sometimes an old friend would land in town and relieve this introspection. One such visit occurred just as Peter felt he was solving the issue of boredom, just as he was pursuing the connection between boredom and self-destruction. Aside from the usual academic work in this line Peter had been reading other less respected but possibly more instructive sources. He'd read a fair amount of Colin Wilson, but just before Sasha turned up he'd been reading a biography of Janice Joplin called *Buried Alive*, by Myra Friedman. Though this was a popular paperback that summer, it was a well-written, thoughtful study — like Mitford's *Zelda* and Charter's *Kerouac* — and it attempted to solve that dangerous passage from lower-middle-class beginnings through to the excesses of money and scapegoat fame, beyond even that to the multifarious boredom and wish to implode that waited at the end of all that. The way Friedman focussed on the debt Joplin felt she owed to her middle-class beginnings, and the guilt she endured about the distance she'd come from those beginnings, struck Peter close to home. He had never felt comfortable in the privileged world he had entered when he pulled himself away from his childhood environment, its beliefs and joys. Instead, he always harked back longingly to the down-to-earth, unpretentious lives of his family and his old friends. Peter wanted it all. He wanted the knowledge of his new, privileged world, but he also wanted the innocence, the self-defeat and irony of his old, less-free world. He understood the contradictions in this greed and saw many examples in the lives around him. It had seemed to him when he lived in Toronto that little of its artistic energy actually surfaced from the city itself. Instead, it was imported from small places in Newfoundland, Manitoba, Alberta. The young people who tried to survive as imports were unprepared for the contradictions involved. They were invariably co-opted by an indolent, privileged group of young people from Toronto. They were either co-opted by that crowd or worn down by a resistance to it, so much so that they collapsed finally into self-indulgence. Their original energy disappeared, and they were left shells of their former selves sitting around in lounges whining about the abuses of privilege. It was an old, old story. These imports could not escape their own innocence, nor the original environments that innocence had been forged in: the lower or middle-class worlds which had given them their energy in the first place and from which they were now banished. Friedman's analysis of Joplin's slow self-destruction merely confirmed these suspicions in Peter. He had just finished underlining this passage from *Buried Alive* when Sasha showed up at the side door for a visit:

"It was not because the praise betrayed a love for the ordinary and unprovocative, which most of it certainly did — everything was fine when Janice was 'just like everybody else.' What bothered me was something much more insidious, a vision of safety, a dreary unevenness beyond which there is unmentionable danger. Then I realised that Janice had held exactly that vision and that she'd been true to her roots 'till the end. She'd gone out and proven it to be absolutely true."

Since she and her first husband Kevin had parted back in 1972, Sasha had been working furiously, and constantly falling in love. Her work proceeded smoothly and professionally, but the love was "a rough and rocky road" and fascinating to hear about. Sasha was never shy about imparting the details of romance to a friendly ear. She was a uniquely confident woman with men because she liked herself: she believed she had a lot to offer and she was right. She'd stand before Peter, shake her thick auburn hair back over her shoulders, pull her sweater tight over her full breasts, and laugh. "How do I look, eh?" she'd shout, mocking herself. She was a beautiful woman who liked men, but found them endlessly exasperating and loved to tell them why.

This time she was especially worried about her new romance with Rob, a fiercely left-wing journalist from Newfoundland. He was living in Vancouver writing a book and working in a factory. He was also a folk-rock singer in his spare time. What Sasha couldn't understand about this guy was his uncanny lack of ambition from her point of view: his inability, it seemed to her, to carry any of his brilliant projects through — either by becoming a first-rate journalist, or by completing his lengthy book which would be, she said, the first legitimate analysis of Canadian political history from a left-wing point of view. Though this man seemed so intense about his projects, so passionate about their importance to him, he drank a bit and complained more about the pretensions of people who *did* complete such things, about the bourgeoise naïveté which allowed them to complete them, him believing that such people would never even be aware of the guts it would take to do *the real thing*, etc etc. Poor Sasha, Peter thought. She must have been treading deep water in this one, and Rob must have been, too, by the sounds of it. As she unravelled it before him, it seemed to Peter to be an almost impossible romance given Rob's Bartleby to her Pollyanna, especially considering her success, which was unavoidable because she was so proud of it. Sasha was a very good photographer. She had shown extensively. She simply couldn't understand why most of the men she knew couldn't get things done like she did.

Peter and Sasha talked a lot about Carol and the novel she was completing in Toronto. They talked about Sasha's last show — a collection of brilliant photographs of poor people in four large Canadian cities. It had been so successful that it had been reviewed in *Maclean's* and *Saturday Night*. She'd shake her head when the subject of Peter's study of Lowry came up, refusing to understand why it wasn't out of the way, easily finished. This caused parallels to emerge in her mind between Peter and her present lover. Rob was resisting Sasha's pushing, too, like an Irishman receiving instructions from a British soldier. It was 1975, after all, and Sasha stood at the forefront of a large group of young Canadian women who were taking the feminist movement seriously, and were tempted to judge men and their problems from that point of view, too, trying to generalise things, lump things together in a common logic. Sasha was, in fact, an accomplished generalist. Her years of photography and journalism had trained her to see wide parallels and quick answers. Peter didn't care much for these sometimes, nor for the conclusions she reached, but he had to admit that he loved listening to Sasha as she worked her way by an uncanny free-association to arrive at them, a curious affection and sincerity in her face as she awaited a response. And now she really *did* want to know what was wrong with all her men. Peter felt for a moment like that character in Graeme Gibson's *Communion* struggling to answer the question his lover asks while he's barfing into the toilet: "What's the matter with you guys, anyway?"

One afternoon Sasha and Peter had gone for a coffee and cheesecake to The Danish Tearoom on Robson. On the way back, wheeling over the Burrard Bridge in her car, hurtling into that gigantic Molson's sign, Peter got excited and tried to explain some things to Sasha. They'd been talking things over in the restaurant but Peter hadn't been able to focus his ambiguous reactions to her theories and questions. Arching over the bridge through its traffic, he tried to explain what it was like for a man to be afraid of being in the wrong movie: how one very important contemporary disease — with its roots in the war, the fifties and the emergence of TV — was that we constantly visualised ourselves acting out roles, were continually seeing ourselves choose and decide things. And how, especially after the late sixties, that watching and seeing precluded certain decisions, ambitions or achievements from being legitimate. It produced a masochistic paralysis which held men back, fixed them forever blinking into cameras. Sasha tried to look interested. She actually looked confused, even confirmed in her theories and how they applied to him. Peter was disappointed. Maybe she was right in the long run.

Later that night, half-way through a bottle of Manor St. David's, Peter wrote a letter to Sasha but never mailed it. He was trying to answer her questions for himself:

Dear Sasha:

I'm sitting here tonight pissed off and not pissed off at the same time. I know you will understand. But I wanted to say some things to you while you were here — as a human, not necessarily as a man — and every time I tried to get something out it seemed I was overwhelmed by a wall of feminist rhetoric from you. It's all very innocent in some ways, I know. But can you imagine how frustrating it is for me? It's one thing to run into simplification of issues out there in our culture. I expect that. So do you. But it's really jarring to run into it on a one-to-one basis. It drives me crazy, of course, makes me cynical. You know me: my twisted sense of humor. But you also know what good friends we have been at times, Sasha. And, knowing that, I want you to understand what it's like to be me when someone like you asks all those questions.

You asked me so many when you were here. Considering what's been happening lately — especially between me and Carol — the implications of some of them are far-reaching. Though I tried my best to answer them for you, I felt that either you weren't really listening to me, or you wanted answers that were clean, that were clear. And I don't think you can afford to believe that they will be clean or clear. It all has to do with the old, old story of how we measure one another, how we perceive success and failure. It's an old story made new by us, by the way we film each other's movies, by the faulty cameras we use.

Sensitive, ambitious women have a clearly defined role to play in our culture right now if they want to play it. It is a generally positive role and meets with approval from all sides: the intellectual elite, the underground politically left elite, the ideologisers, if all that's real. I mean, if all those audiences are there, in fact. And I guess they are. In other words, you have stumbled onto the perfect spot on the stage, would have trouble making any mistakes there given these liberal, generally insecure audiences. The equally sensitive man's role, on the other hand, is under

fire from all sides and almost every alternative for sane and
impassioned action is questionable or undermined in advance. Fair enough, I know. It has been rotten for women
forever. I know. In men right now, I see a great subterranean fear of 'having the wrong dream' or, as I mentioned
to you in the car, of 'being in the wrong movie,' the latter
being superficial compared to the former. And it's a good
thing, this fear. We need it. But as a result there is also a
marked inability to perform, to realise faltering ambitions
in the face of it. Sour grapes, you say. Fair enough in one
way. But deeper than that. The men I know who have
chosen clearly-defined, simplified routes to success are
envied by the rest of us who take predictable refuge in what
appears to be superiority. But it's just that we can't function
smoothly like that, can't create advertisements for self like
that. Also, to give us some credit, those other men have
simplified the route, so much so that I can't approve of it,
or live with it, or live like that. I want something else,
naturally, something better, whatever that might be. I wish
I knew.

Last night was a fine example of this. There we were with
Rob and Gene and the band dumping on guys like Bruce
Miller just because Bruce is smart enough to simplify his
talents, to streamline them so that they scream out for
success and get it, get resounding applause from people
like you, Sasha. Might as well admit it. He gets this approval for the deed done publicly — public being so fucking
important these days. When I walked out on that conversation, I wasn't mad at Rob and Gene, but at the paradox
they're caught in right now: two talented guys feeling done
in by their envy for another guy who can do something
they can't seem to do: sell himself; package himself. I hate
it when I feel like that, too. I think it's an important thing
to hate actually. I mean it.

Over the past twenty years a combination of magazine,
television and movie images has amassed unwittingly to
create the cruel slavery of the ordinary person to ideal
images of action — moral, or immoral or amoral, doesn't
really matter. The aegis of the media. Your line, Sasha.
Hype. Instead of acting in a situation, or acting out a

situation, the instant reflex is to visualise that action: to watch ourselves act. To compare ourselves hopelessly to ideal images of action imposed upon us by all that junk and cunningly false dreaming that sells things and allows people like us to become decadent enough and privileged enough to even consider these issues. This is a complex truth. The paralysis of a very real, technologically induced self-consciousness. As a result, we are once-removed from immediate experience, literally beside ourselves. We want to be the hero or the heroine in our own movie and be able to watch it, too. An insane, insecure Job sitting on a stinking dungheap with his video pack, squatting on that pile of shit created by man's visualisation of himself, by our society's absurd faith in false ideals — platonic selves rather than real selves; magazine, television and movie selves rather than the wonderful, fumbling creatures we really are. That's why you're so full of disappointments, Sasha, and why you have so many frustrating questions. You're attracted to certain guys who resist these false ideals, and then you wonder why they can't turn into one of those romantic ads in Esquire or New Yorker for Christ's sake. We have to accept our own roles in this whole process: we are the generation, we greedy baby-boomers, who began this step into abstraction. It began innocently enough: we rebelled against the 'Father Knows Best' world of our parents. Their false ideals of marriage etc etc. But we've trapped ourselves now, extended our movies to include our own adult scripts: what a divorce should look like, how the pain of a destroyed marriage should be played out for fuck's sake. All these movies. Stop all these movies. Neither the slick, photographed propaganda of the right or the left reflects, answers or applies to the day-to-day textures of immediate experience. Instead, it betrays them to a ridiculous, liberal movie of self-visualisation which is loathsome, and in the end, pathetic.

This is why our society loses the benefit of some initially committed people who might try to redirect us from some of this because they see it, understand it. Ironically, their energy is deflected into negative energy: bitterness, and the painful self-knowledge that even though they themselves are to blame for their failures, there seem no alternatives. These sit around in bars and lounges, and long for love. Or they kill themselves. And most cruel, they are the first ones to be accused of a misguided romanticism, are patronised and dismissed on that ground. We call them romantics: failed idealists, soft-hearted cynics, burn-outs. Roberta Flack singing "All The Sad Young Men." So they must endure this final humiliation when they might be the only people who function in and resist this void: our culture defined by its lack of romanticism on the one hand, but by its prostrating itself utterly before a more insidious kind of romanticism, visualised all around itself, on the other.

In more bitter arguments, I have often been accused of trying to write myself into a movie of romantic self-destruction inspired by my literary heroes. My heroes have always been cowboys. "Hey! That's why Peter's working on Malcolm Lowry. It all makes sense now. Too bad, eh? He had such promise, too!" Henry Tremblechin selling pencils on the street corner in the last frame. And, believe me, that is the last frame in every sense of that word. There are some unbearable ironies in your view of whatever paralysis you suspect I have, Sasha. First, I do not want to repeat Lowry's life any more than I want to repeat my father's pain. Second, Lowry understood what was happening to him and wrote about that ruthlessly in the sincere hope, I think, that by writing about it he might understand the problem in himself — which he also saw as the world's problem — and save both himself and the world in the process. How pompous of him! And yet his vision is continually patronized. Think about it. People don't read his novels. But they love his biography, drawn to the scene of some alcoholic accident like flies to a honeyed movie they want to see but forget about quickly afterwards. I don't know how many answers Gibson's heroine wanted to hear in that bathroom scene in 'Communion', but it returns all this to your question: "What's the matter with you guys, anyway?" Well, what's the matter with you for Christ's sake? Read and watch more. Take fewer pictures. Stare North America in its heart.

Shit, Sasha. You understand what I'm trying to say even if
I haven't said it right. I'll drop you a line and let you know
when I'm coming through Edmonton. Probably in early
September. Take care.

Peter walked over to Rohan's after he'd completed that
letter. He wanted to get plastered. He was mad. Not at Sasha,
but at their world. A group of friends from Nelson blew in
the door delighted to discover him drinking. Peter left,
walked down to the bench near the beach and watched the
carnival-lighted ships list far out in the bay like waltzing
chandeliers, the twinkling lights of Eden.

Two days later he picked up a few more Colin Wilson
books and some west-coast poetry down in Richard Pender's
Bookstore. As he ascended onto the street he found a fifty-
year-old woman in trouble. She was slumping down the
rough bricks to the sidewalk.

Her mauve dress was damp with sweat. She was suffering
a serious attack of D.T.'s. Peter helped her home. Two other
people pitched in, too, and they arrived at her place without
having to call an ambulance, a move she was frightened
they'd make. When Peter had first leaned down to talk to her
it had turned out that he'd taught her son in Nelson. She told
him that Sam was doing really well now in Vernon. This
seemed a predictable coincidence to Peter. His life was full
of them. Misery likes company as J.J. Cale sings of Clyde and
his dog.

Peter read Colin Wilson for different reasons. He'd read
The Outsider years back and had been impressed by Wilson's
ability to generalise. A voice for the layman, Peter had decided. He'd also read a few of Wilson's novels beginning
with *The God of the Labyrinth*. He'd found that piece erotic,
though as Carol pointed out to him quite fiercely, it was
typically sexist, the plot literally climaxing around the hero's
inexhaustible penis. Peter had liked those passages a lot but
he kept quiet about them. He'd thought, cynically, that it was
all right for Erica Jong to create a similar effect in *Fear of*

Flying; in fact, it was *important* for her to achieve it, as long as
the woman was the selfish heroine. But in Wilson it was
inexcusable. He was a man. Peter had also enjoyed some of
Wilson's science fiction though in the end he'd dismissed it
because the plots were such thin structures upon which
Wilson aired his increasingly strident philosophical convic-
tions. On his earnest quest to understand boredom, however,
Peter had just read *Beyond The Outsider* and another smaller
book called *Hesse, Reich and Borges.* In the former Wilson
attacked and explored the issue of intentionality: the pressure of consciousness. This issue fascinated Peter because it
seemed to him that it was at the heart of the mystery of
boredom. According to Wilson, western culture created a
sensibilty that couldn't experience intentionality. Instead, it
was a sensibility obsessed by the surfaces of things, and
restless when experience ceased to be kinetic and it had to
stop and actually probe into what was before it. This inability
to probe, to reach the essence of things, caused a boredom if
experience was forced into it. As a result, western sensibility
had to keep moving, be constantly stimulated. In recom-
mending the experience of intentionality, leaning heavily on
the long eastern traditions of approaching life in this way,
Wilson outlined a process by which a person could achieve
it. Even though he mulled this over and over, Peter knew
instinctively that there was something askew in Wilson's
process: though it sounded great, there was something about
it that bothered Peter. *If such stillness were the garden it
promised to be.* Eventually, one night when he was sitting over
in Rohan's listening to the Cement City Cowboys — a group
drunkenly ahead of its time — Peter wrote a letter to Wilson,
another missive he couldn't mail:

Dear Mr. Wilson:

What I'm writing you about is the issue of intentionality as
you raise it in *Beyond The Outsider.* It seems to me that on a
personal level my continuing difficulties have been caused
by a resistance to my self-self-consciousness all my life:
seeing it as a demobilising disease which I had somehow

to harness and accommodate. Either that, or it seemed difficult to live easily with the people around me. You have helped create a release from this obsessive self-denial. I realise — albeit imperfectly — that my own intentionality is a virtue rather than a vice in me. But you make one assumption — and it is widely and falsely made in our culture — that bothers me: you seem to feel that most ordinary men and women, dulled by distraction, do not have a high quotient of intentionality, or more simply, pressure of consciousness. I think you are dangerously wrong there. In fact, I believe that most ordinary people have, as the pivotal point in their day-to-day joy and frustration, a vortex of self-self-consciousness the meaning of which might elude them as it has me, but which is, still, their deepest life.

It seems to me now that my problem was that instead of seeing this intentionality as my base of existence, and facing it, I have tried to abstract its processes in some way in order to survive them. The other night, for example, I went down and sat on a bench in the harbor to watch the sun set into the vast, careless bay. I enjoyed the visual and emotional context of this scene. I understood. The evil or destructive side of this experience was my objectification of it: that is, my automatic reflex to see myself sitting there watching the scene instead of simply being there. In some way this objectification seemed a necessary part of the pressure of the experience. In another way, however, I believe it was the weakest part. It is just this impulse to objectify which is the last link in the chain of our inherited, evolving intellectual processes. Naturally, the increasingly manipulative technologies of TV and film feed this impulse and provide specific visual models against which we judge ourselves, our objectified selves. Terrified by a sense of large audiences, we objectify ourselves pointlessly into roles and in the process lose what would otherwise be our legitimate pressure of consciousness. I agree that we are not easy with intentionality, that we avoid it because we see in it the source of boredom and terror; we are a culture that cannot afford to be still, that strives for mutability because we fear its opposite. But I still believe that this stillness is in us, that intentionality does not have to be something we work towards. In fact, your view of the objective "way" to intentionality encourages an outward rather than an inward journey, pushes us farther in the direction of our sick love of nothing but movement, our perverted obeisance to object rather than subject. Our biggest mistake is to assume that the nature of the experience of intentionality is, somehow, a "still" experience when it has to be in motion, too — like we are — and only still in the way Eliot defined stillness in 'Four Quartets'. If we could accept this paradox our surface movement could be comforted into real intentionality: the ability to survive in the heart of that paradox.

Intentionality is not something we need to approach, or learn how to achieve, but something we need to accept in our lives because it is already there.

Sincerely,

Not surprisingly, Peter still got bored often, but the reading and a few letters like that one helped him out, made him feel he was getting somewhere. And he walked. He walked Kitsilano until he knew it intimately, until he felt part of its confused green insistence that aside from West Broadway it would remain what it was: a 1930's pastoral. The rich diversion of looking at things, getting lost in the detailed life of things, helped both his work and his restlessness. One Sunday night Peter went out for one of his longest walks, eventually stopping at the closed doors of Rohan's to read all the posters, discover who'd start on Monday night.

They were hiring great groups that summer and even on a Monday night the place could be so packed you'd have to stand. It was a good idea to be prepared in order to get a seat. A lot of deals went down in Rohan's. It was a natural dispensary in that sense, the deals concluded in the darker corners or in the cans. Suddenly, as Peter was standing there gazing, a cab pulled up to the curb beside him and deposited a man who was a bit older than Peter and who, though he looked more stylish, more sophisticated on the one hand, looked a bit thin, somewhat burnt-out on the other. The arrival leapt at the double doors to the club nervously and began banging and pulling their handles. He turned around and faced Peter thinking that Peter must be the owner of the club.

"What's the fuckin' scam, man?"

Peter realised that this guy was out of it. "It's Sunday," he replied. "They're closed."

The man rolled his eyes upwards, then turned his head suddenly to stare down the street and back again at Peter more fiercely. "It can't be fuckin' *closed* man! . . . What the *fuck* are you trying to *lay* on me anyways?"

Peter felt oddly responsible. "Sorry. I was just walking by, looking at the posters . . . "

"I don't give a *shit* what *you* were looking at, dude . . . I was supposed to meet the man . . . the *man*, man . . . tonight . . . *tonight!*"

"Well, I'm sorry," Peter offered.

"Fuck this fuckin' *shit!* I mean *shit*, man!" At this point the would-be customer proceeded to kick the metal bike stand over and over again with his thin Italian shoes. Peter could still hear him half a block away until, quite suddenly, the agony ceased. He must have got a new idea, Peter thought, figured out some new angle, flagged down another cab. But the man standing there, kicking his metal world impossibly, wanting something so badly from it made Peter's own restlessness seem like a medieval trance: made Peter feel lucky.

One Tuesday afternoon in mid-August Peter was sitting with a coffee in SUB when he decided to leave Vancouver. That day. Pull out and begin the long haul back to Toronto through Nelson, Calgary, Edmonton, and Lloydminster. It seemed wonderfully simple. He merely cleaned up the loose ends at the bank and headed home to fill up the Datsun. It took him until 7:00 p.m. to get all this done. He didn't bother going up to talk to the landlady. It was pointless. Another of

the sleasier melodramas had begun in earnest around 5:00
p.m. and was just reaching its crescendo by the time Peter
was ready to leave. He left a note with some money in it.

All afternoon, while Peter had carted boxes, laundry bags
and suitcases out to his car, the next-door neighbour was
throwing his own unique party in his yard. Chester Duncan
had hounded the neighborhood all summer long. He was
obsessed by order in things. He drove a one-ton truck which
he parked in front of his home every night. Once or twice he
had given Peter shit for parking the Datsun one or two inches
over onto his property line. Peter had ignored the brush-
cutted little asshole which was fun because Duncan seemed
to have — or thought he had — a tight rein on the street, a
mess officer's final say. He would kick dogs regularly, yell at
children, or imitate, in his own imagined sense of precision,
an East Indian accent when Sam would come home or when
an East Indian family would stroll by. Duncan would sit
there on his porch every night, just fifteen yards from Peter's
screened window, and grumble about anything, looking for
a fight, fuelling himself with bottle after bottle of beer. It was
nauseating. He was a bitter man. He must have suffered
something big to have turned into what he was now: a bigot
who'd lost his brains years back in some sad act of terminal
anger and pain. Just as Peter had tucked his guitar into its
special place in the backseat of the Datsun, an encounter took
place that saved him, made him laugh all the way to Nelson.

Duncan had just finished mowing his lawn. He'd put
away the mower in his back shed and was beginning to
arrange a series of sprinklers throughout his garden — sneer-
ing sideways at the unkempt lawns around him — when the
landlady's daughter surfaced onto her back patio deck in her
housecoat, a bottle of Scotch dangling from one veined hand.
She proceeded to deliver the precise kind of order Chester
Duncan deserved from his world.

"You have wronged me and many others, Chester
Duncan," she began, "you little turd with the brain of a

hamster." Her speech was insane. It pivoted around her suspicion that Duncan had been poisoning her cats — a notion which was, in fact, not that paranoid considering what he was capable of. "You hate yourself and everyone else in this world."

The fascinating thing about their encounter for Peter was that while her chaotic howling increased, Duncan's blushing fastidiousness around the yard increased, too. Duncan disappeared into his garden shed. It became clear that the landlady's daughter *had* something on this guy. Watching Duncan's reluctance to respond, Peter wondered whether the man was actually afraid of her, but that seemed impossible. Unbelievable. Then Peter noticed that the insanity of her speech had shifted into something else: a sheer logic that exists sometimes at the far end of pain. "That is why you sneak over here sometimes and beg me to make love to you while your wife sleeps." She set the bottle down near some begonias and stretched her arms wide as if signifying the breadth of the audience she suspected was paying close attention to her. She allowed the housecoat to open and fall to her feet in one graceful motion. She stood there naked, her body ravaged by its history of anger, and stretched her arms out again to indicate the pain she was embracing around her. "And I have. I have satisfied you because I have been drunk and lonely." She seemed mythical to Peter, as if she had arrived magically as some emblem of life to administer balsam to this suburb crouching in its trees and fears. And like a strong breeze that lifts a whole neighborhood to a crisp chattering of leaves, her voice began, sure of itself, almost biblical.

"I am often drunk and lonely. But you should know that you do not fool me. You are a horrible person. There is little to redeem you. So I announce today that as lonely as I am, as confused as I sometimes get in the booze, I will no longer love you. You have poisoned my cats. You are beyond repair. We

are all watching you now. You have lost your power over us.
We will not put up with you."

Duncan appeared for a moment in the doorframe of his
shed, a wild, unbelieving glare in his eyes. He glanced up at
this apparition standing naked above him and scuttled into
the safety of his kitchen, the anonymity of his phone.

"He is phoning the police now," she resumed. "We have
won." For a fraction of a second the landlady's daughter's
face smiled into the sun. "*Consummatum est.*" And she disappeared into her kitchen.

As she glided through the sliding glass doors, Peter could
hear, faintly at first, then clearly all around him, the sound
of clapping. The whole neighborhood was in on this. From
behind one shuttered window, someone yelled, "Right on!"
From another, "Like you can, sister!" The whole suburb
seemed to come alive with approval. Peter stood there in the
middle of this applause, trying to understand it. The police
car pulled up just as Peter was pulling away from this
forever.

He drove straight through to Nelson, through those clear,
crisp stars, stopping only for gas, coffee and a short nap off
the highway outside of Greenwood. Cradled by fifty-foot
ponderosa pines near a picnic table, the sounds of semis
coming and going in his ears, Peter dreamed. In one dream
Peter was happy. He was sitting somewhere and he was
surprised because he wasn't doing anything and he felt
happy. It was so beautiful just sitting there. Then he realised
that someone was with him. His forehead was pressed
against the forehead of the landlady's daughter. Her skin was
soft and he realised that she was smiling back at him, looking
through him, peacefully. Peter had never felt so happy and
he started to cry, a great heaving release that was both painful
and wonderful at the same time. It was love. She understood
and they didn't have to say anything, to think anything, to
name anything. Then he realised that the eyes he was seeing
through were her eyes and he decided he should try to see

what they were seeing. So he looked through the web of veins and dark colors and he could feel her smiling somewhere as these eyes filled with trees and grass and wonderful scraps of white paper and sometimes the pocked bright surfaces of fruit, pebbled oranges, leathery pears. It was the world he had begun to eat and see and love and as he began to tumble somehow into the blinding colour of it he cried even more deeply for the pain of it, the joy. It was like falling through layer after layer into something that never ended. It was wonderful.

It was over. Peter had been drooling onto a spot on the passenger seat. Fractured sunlight descended through the pine needles. A semi brushed by. It was a new day. He whipped the car out over the gravel and onto the highway.

_____ I'm Not Like Merv, Helen

1.

Bendy's face had that look on it again. It was a half-lidded drop of muscles into boredom. A predictable re-arrangement of jowls into a fixed stare of resignation. A private answer to the world. He only allowed himself to slip into it in front of mirrors, to "Merv Griffin" late at night if he was by himself, or like now, into the peeling white surface of the half-opened back door.

"And if you can remember this time, why don't you finally go in and make a blessed appointment to see Dr. Cowley?" she shouted down the stairs to him over the sound of the radio blaring.

"Sure," Bendy replied to his uneven fingernail.

"Oh. And pick me up some fresh chicken legs at Safeway?"

"Yeah."

"We'll have them for supper."

"Sure."

"You won't be too long this time?"

"Don't think so."

Bendy drew the door toward himself, then hesitated. "Well. I might be about an hour. Going to go to the bank, too." And closed the door quickly, like the period he would have put there. He rounded the corner of the house, approached his car, felt his hand grasp the handle, open the door. "Shove it up your goddamn arsehole," he whispered to the steering-wheel as he checked out his victorious smile in the rear-view mirror and backed out of the driveway.

2.

Bendy drove his 1969 Chevy Nova down 118th Avenue to the Simpson Sears shopping plaza. He was proud of his car. He had just washed it Saturday and it gave him pleasure to think that it was only three years old.

Carly Wholer, standing waiting for the bus to arrive, was thinking about last night when Tom had finally touched her "down there" as he'd put it. She smiled to herself as she remembered the delirious, pathetic look on his face and the way he had grasped her hand in time and placed it with a groan on his pants. On his knob.

Carly took a seat near the back and stared out the window, her fingers folding and unfolding the white uniform she would put on when she got to Safeway for the afternoon shift. Directly opposite her sat two elderly women, Eunice and Angela. They were congratulating one another about small things: walking to the bus stop, getting up the stairs, having the exact change, finding a seat, having enough money to go shopping, and the kind of day it was today, how last year had been so cold, and so on. At the next stop an equally old immigrant woman, wearing a polka-dotted kerchief and hockey socks, tumbled by them from the back seat of the bus. She whined something frantic to the bus driver, and in a paroxysm of sighs and grunts, managed to release the bus doors at the next stop and fall, whimpering, into the street. "Edmonton has certainly changed," Eunice declared to the bright stainless steel on the back of the seat in front of her. "Hasn't it though?" Angela agreed as she adjusted the ankle nylons stuffed into her shoes.

Carly looked across at these two and thought to herself, why don't you two fart out the rest of your brains and call it a life. She checked the inside of the uniform's collar the same instant that Bendy forgot about going to the bank and turned into the plaza parking lot instead. One of the elderly women, Eunice, the one on the left in the checkered coat, coughed once and suppressed a belch. It's that darn fake orange juice,

she decided. Probably hadn't even felt one before, Carly
smiled to herself.

3.

Bendy backed out one more time to give it another try. The
unexpected blast of a horn made him jump in his seat. A
young man with long dark hair glared angrily at him from
the Volkswagen he had almost hit and which was now
lurching backward to give him more room. "All right,
buddy," Bendy whispered to the curve of the upholstery,
"Take it easy." As he eased his car into the space successfully
this time, he caught a glimpse of the Volkswagen and its
angry driver piling out of the parking lot, squealing its tires
as it turned into the exit lane. Somehow the fierceness of the
car and its driver drained Bendy, made his hands tremble.
Made him wonder why, after having been a reasonable guy
all his life, people constantly used him in this way now. For
a moment he imagined himself with a machine gun, mowing
both car and driver to shreds. A lot of people who looked
very much like himself were clapping and congratulating
him afterward. Then he felt badly about that, too. As he
locked the car and glanced over at the shopping plaza, he
experienced a touch of vertigo. I'm having another bad day,
damn it.

"Some of those old pricks should have their cars taken
away."

"Come on, Dick. You don't . . ."

"He almost hit us!"

"Well, maybe he didn't see . . ."

"HE ALMOST HIT US. PERIOD. OK?"

"OK, OK."

Carly slipped into her uniform in the stockroom just as
Eunice and Angela were reading the floor directory sign to
see where they could find notions. "That's what I like about

Southgate," said Angela, "Everything's on the main floor there." Eunice clucked for both of them, "We'll have to ask, I guess."

After he'd passed through the entrance Bendy noticed an attractive young woman dressed in a long, flowered dress. He noticed her because she was smiling at him, and approaching him with her two hands raised. One held a daffodil and the other a long straightpin. "Hello, sir. Today is men's flower day and I want you to wear this free daffodil."

"But I . . ."

"Our group runs four religious camps in Guatemala, and we want you to know about us, and wear this free flower." She grinned genuinely while she took hold of Bendy's sportcoat and pinned a flower in its left lapel, her knee brushing his as she did so. Bendy felt weak and also couldn't help noticing the bare curve of a breast showing through the loose folds of her flowered dress. She smiled sorrowfully at him. "We rely on kind people like yourself to help us to keep our camps going . . ."

"But, you said . . ."

"If all the peoples of the world could see, as I'm sure that you see, that sharing is the only way we can begin to confront. . ."

"You said the flower was *free!*"

"We only ask that you . . ."

"That it was *free!*"

"A small amount if you could spare . . ."

"I don't have a red cent. I'm sorry."

The beautiful young woman stared at him for a second. Then he felt her hands on his lapel and looked vaguely at her as she removed the flower and walked away.

Barry Knight, stockboy, pinched Carly's behind as she passed by him through the clapping, thin aluminum doors. She yelled *Barry!* at him and, flushed, rounded the frozen food counter and disappeared. God, I'd like to screw the ass off her, he thought. And he had to reach into one pocket to rearrange his penis which was caught, getting hard, on the wrong angle.

I love these hot dogs, Bendy thought. He was sitting beside the Wonky Food Stand eating one of their foot-long specials. Enjoying every bite. Especially when they put out those shredded onions. In the middle of his next bite, he looked over and spotted the flower girl approaching some- one else at the entrance. He saw how pretty she was, and he felt angry again, felt his vertigo return, threw the rest of the hot dog into the garbage bin next to him, and burped silently to himself. His heart pounding.

"On the second floor, ladies, behind the escalator."

4.

Ascending symbolism. Descending symbolism. I think I've got it, Peter thought, and he placed the book down on the terry-towel for a moment and signalled Jimmy for two more beers. *The Inward Turn of the Narrative*, by Erich Kahler. The book even looked important and after his first four draft, Peter was convinced that what Kahler was getting at was something that he himself had been coming to intuitively and hadn't yet expressed. Here I am, he thought. I'm only twenty- two and I'm on the right track. All this made him feel good. I'm feeling good, he thought.

"Reading again, eh?"

"Yeah."

"It's as good a place as any to do that I guess."

"Yeah." Peter handed Jimmy the dollar. "Keep the change Jimmy."

"Thanks kid."

5.

"Excuse me?"

"Yes?"

"Sorry to bother you."

"No problem."

"But do you have any *thawed* chicken breasts?"

"No way."

"Well, the ones here, these frozen ones . . . how long . . ."

"Have 'em for supper. No sweat."

"Really?"

"Thaw fast. Small."

"Right."

Bendy hated feeling the fool like this, but he just couldn't be sure. And he didn't want Helen whining when he got home. So he picked up the package of four chicken breasts and headed down the aisle, past all the turkeys and the hams, turned the corner where all the different pickles were, and got angry when he saw how long the express line was. The fat woman in front of him, decked out in a tartan jumpsuit, seemed to be thinking the same thing, too, for she looked at him, rolled her eyes, pursed her lipstick at the young cashier caustically, and then looked back at him with a half-smile.

"I know," he said.

He noticed that she was lugging a five-pound bag of kitty litter. She noted his notice, then smiled. "For my cat." They both nodded, conspiratorially. Afterward she glanced out the window and he examined the chicken breasts carefully.

6.

Eunice didn't care to be patronised like this, but she knew, too, that Angela's shyness would prevent their getting satisfaction. That was precisely what she intended to get as she

faced this young woman who was leaning toward her over
the counter of candies and chocolates. Appearing rather
bored, Eunice thought. But all the same. "But you certainly
used to," she announced crisply.

"Well, I guess so ma'am. I guess we . . ."

"Well. I can't imagine why you would cease to carry them.
The Bay downtown . . ."

"What did you say the brand was?"

Eunice looked at Angela for some support and raised her
voice inadvertently, spitting out the syllables, turning herself
into the caricature she suspected this young girl to have
drawn of her. "*Callard and Bowser's.* They make *eight* lines of
toffee and nougat in pretty colored, tiny boxes, wrapped in
cellophane."

"Yes, well . . ."

"I simply can't understand it."

"Well, I'm sorry ma'am. But I know we don't stock that
brand."

"You certainly *should.* And you won't be getting our business anymore I can tell you."

"I'm sorry."

"Yes."

As Eunice and Angela turned away together, the young
girl shared eye contact with a young male customer who
smiled sadly and said, "Can get awful cranky."

"I know."

7.

"Chicken breasts. A dollar sixty-eight." Probably never felt
or saw one before.

"Miss?"

"Yes?"

"Could you put the chicken breasts in *two* bags?"

"We don't normally double-bag items that . . ."

"Could melt."

"Yes."

"Thanks."

"Yes."

And you can double-bag my itemed arsehole while you're at it, Bendy thought. Like to say that to her tight little nose and mouth.

8.

Bendy's was the first car to stop for the red light. He slipped the automatic shift into park as he always did at a light. Someone had told him he'd save on gas that way. He glanced over at the chicken breasts on the passenger seat and noticed a stain appearing beneath the package on the upholstery. He reached over frantically to place the bag on the floor when the car behind him honked, and instead of placing it there gently, his hands leapt and the bag flew to the floor with a thud. He caught the driver's eyes in the rear-view mirror and gunned his accelerator. This time the guy behind him leaned on his horn forever until Bendy realised his mistake, shifted into drive, and lurched forward across the intersection. The car behind him swerved like a knife into the lane beside him and Bendy caught sight of the raised finger before the car accelerated and left him behind. I'll go down to the Legislature Park for a bit, he thought, as if speaking this gently to the combination of his thumping heart and growing nausea. I'll go to the park for a bit. But where are all these buggers coming from today, he asked himself. And then yelled over the steering wheel, "I *know*. I *know*. But I'm an OK guy for Christ's sake!"

9.

Bendy sat on the varnished pine bench facing the river valley. He could hear below him the steady traffic moving along the River Road. Other than that, and the soft contradictory muffle of the sounds of downtown behind him, it was quiet. For some reason he thought about the times he'd walked up to the Greenhill Lookout near his home in Nova Scotia. When he was a boy. And how that seemed such a special time now, looking back on it. Kind of stupid to think that, he thought, because I wasn't thinking that then. Just having a good time. Probably worried about whether the worms'd dry up before I got down to the creek to fish. Probably picking my nose or something. Still, the sunlit movie played itself mischievously before him. The dappled trees and a soft breeze from Pictou. All kinds of hope, he thought. All kinds.

Then he noticed the couple lying beneath the big maple about a hundred yards to his right. The long-haired young man looked familiar, but was lying on his side, one hand linked behind his head which was facing away from Bendy. It was his son, Peter. His girlfriend Carol sat beside him holding her knees with both arms, rocking back and forth on her behind. Neither of them could see Bendy. She put a hand under her long skirt to scratch her leg above her boots while Peter leaned over suddenly and talked to her. Bendy could hear him now, so he decided to stare across the river instead.

"I know I can do it."

"Far out."

"No. Do you see what I'm saying?"

"Well . . ."

"I know I can write it."

"Because of Kahler's book?"

"It's not just the book. What he's saying is something I've been getting at for a long time now but nobody's been understanding in me."

"You've had a lot of beer."

"Jesus Christ! Listen to that will you! Big fucking deal. You don't understand me at all. Beer! Jesus Fucking Christ!"

"Come on, Peter . . ."

"Look! I can do it, and I know that now."

"I believe you Peter."

"No. You don't."

"I *do!*"

Bendy couldn't help looking over at them now. She leaned down to Peter to kiss him, and his hand reached down to the bottom of her dress and moved up her thigh until her soft, round and white behind showed. She's not wearing any panties, Bendy muttered to himself, and turned once more to examine the skyline on the south side. All the new apartments there.

"Hey *Dad!* What the hell are you doing here?"

10.

Bendy poured himself a rye in the kitchen, then swallowed a good gulp from the bottle before he concealed it again behind the J-Cloths under the sink. He could hear Helen moving around upstairs getting ready for bed. When he walked into the den he could hear "The Merv Griffin Show" starting up and his heart sank. But there was also that old challenge, too, as he eased himself into his chair and placed the drink on the coffee table beside it. Bendy enjoyed predicting what Merv would say before he said it and surprised and annoyed Helen with his accuracy.

Merv was grinning and rubbing his hands now as the audience cheered and applauded him. He'd just finished slaughtering Sinatra's "Strangers in the Night" by going flat on the long notes at the end of the phrases. He didn't seem

to care about that. But Bendy did. And I know when someone's off-key, he thought.

"How's everyone feeling tonight?"

"How's everyone feeling tonight?"

"Having a good time?"

"Are you having a great time?"

"We've got lots of . . ."

"We have a terrific line-up . . ."

"Terrific guests . . ."

"Really terrific guests . . ."

"For you tonight."

"For you tonight."

Merv stood gleefully, rocking back and forth on his heels
as he announced his list playfully. Bendy's face had that look
again as he took another long sip. He heard Helen coming
down the stairs.

"And a very special guest will be with us later, too. A
novelist you've all heard about. Yes! J.P. Donleavey will be
with us later to discuss his new book."

The Onion Men. No. What was it again? *Onion Beatitudes?*
No. Bendy had read one of this man's books. It had been
about New York City and the hero's name had been Christian
something. He had laughed a lot when he'd read it, and had
loved the rolling, lilting language that reminded him of how
his Irish grandmother had told him stories. There was a
scene, too. That's it. Something about this hero being called
a goddamn bum by someone. Quite a few times. Called a
faggot, too. Bendy remembered the scene. Finally, the hero
had risen up and threatened to rip the yelling man's balls off,
and he had spoken as if he were a king, or Winston Churchill
on a good day. It had been very funny.

The toilet flushed, and he heard Helen sigh. She peeked
around the corner and shook her head playfully. An old

smiling conspiracy between them. "Why don't you come to bed?"

"Gonna watch Merv."

"Well, don't have another drink."

"OK. No."

"I put the chicken breasts out to thaw."

"I know dear."

"We'll have them tomorrow."

"I *asked* the guy a million times."

"I know."

So Bendy waited. Through a long talk with Debbie Reynolds. Through another long talk with some big fat woman he was supposed to recognise but didn't. A young, nervous comedian came out, but he wasn't very funny. All about when he'd been a kid in high school and how he'd tried to get dates. Same old stuff, Bendy thought. And he did sneak out into the kitchen, and by coughing loudly and running the tap full blast, he managed to pour himself another gigantic rye and have a full blast from the bottle, too, without hearing any moves from upstairs. He returned to his chair and finally, after a long cutesy chat with the earnest guy who played Baretta, Merv announced that after the next commercial J.P. Donleavy would be out to discuss his new book.

The commercial was for Stay-Free Minipads. Two girls were talking about good and bad pads while they were driving in a car. The confident one, who was much prettier than the other one, always used Stay-Free Minipads, she said, for her light days. Bendy couldn't believe it. Why don't they just move the camera in he said aloud to himself and have one of them slap the thing on there for all of us to see? Jesus. And he drained another long dram.

Merv's hands held up a glossy book and the camera moved in on it. "Here it is, folks. The new novel you've all

heard about. And its author, a very dear friend to all of us
here, would you *please* welcome *Mr.! J.! P.! Donleavy!"*

The audience clapped and the camera panned back to get
the whole stage. A tall, bearded, very serious looking man in
his fifties walked over to the chair closest to Merv's and sat
down. He was wearing a grey suit and was carrying a black
cane. Merv was grinning nervously, bobbing his head to the
applause, and so were his other guests, but Donleavy's face
was stone serious, and he didn't smile. Ever.

"Gee . . . well . . . a lot of us are wondering . . . what's it
like to be a famous writer?"

"It is a living, as you people say, and provides one with
certain . . . amenities. Certain . . . mobilities."

"Yes . . . yes?"

"Well, what exactly are you asking me?"

"Well . . . we've all heard that you have . . . what? . . . a
castle in Ireland?"

"It's not a castle."

"But, that you have a fancy place there, and also that
you've just bought a place here, too? In California?"

"That's true."

"Well . . . whaddya think of California?"

"Oh, I . . ."

"Like it better than Ireland . . . huh?"

"No, I . . ."

"What do you like doing here?"

"I like walking around in the graveyards."

Merv looked quizzically out into his audience, inducing
a bond between them and against this guest.

"Yes. I quite like walking around the graveyards because
they're so quiet, and such real symbols for what happens
here. In California you see. In America."

Bendy was crying, softly. Why am I crying, he wondered, so stupid. Happening more and more these days. But his book was so funny, so gentle. God, it was funny. And he's mad on there. And I want him to talk to me because I'm sitting here, and I read his book, and he doesn't have to think I'm like Merv. I'm not.

Bendy knocked back the rest of his rye and leaned forward to turn off the TV. He had stopped crying and merely had that look on his face again. For a few moments he watched Merv and Donleavy with the sound down and imagined what they were saying. He could tell by Merv's nervous grins and winks at his audience that the interview was not going well. Donleavy's expression never changed. Why don't you smile, Bendy thought, and turned the thing off.

The Incredible Mix

The late sixties moved some young people out to edges that hadn't existed before in North America. These edges had always existed, of course, but it had been difficult until then to move beyond them. Peter had grown up in a time of privilege and that made all the difference. One of the privileges was the opportunity to risk the territory outside the conventional life which had carried him this far. There were prices to be paid out there, however, and Peter and others like him found themselves trying to preserve routes back into safety, into the past. When he returned to Toronto in the fall of 1975, Peter lived on such an edge and struggled with it until an old friend made him stare it down for what it was.

In early September Peter arrived at Carol's apartment on Brunswick Avenue. He'd driven non-stop from Edmonton and a summer of drifting in Vancouver. He'd spent it working at UBC, living in a small flat in Kitsilano after quitting his teaching post in Nelson. His decision to quit was deliberate. It was clear to him that the university was going to be closed down in time. It was an opportune moment to get out, in fact. He also realised that he couldn't live in Nelson anymore. His life there had become a shaky pattern of interwoven self-indulgences. It had been an ecstatic and even dignified pattern for a while, but in the last stretch had devolved into different kinds of ruin. He'd moved too far out beyond the edges and had to struggle to get back from them somehow. He was drinking heavily and for this release, a far corner of his consciousness was grateful: he had always been too earnest, too apologetic about his life, too aware of different audiences. But other corners were bent on survival and knew what to do. And something else had happened unexpectedly in Nelson to change things.

Slowly and suddenly, in all the mysterious ways these things seem to happen, he had fallen in love again and was surprised to discover that someone had fallen in love with him, too. Sarah was a student in his literature class. He had been aware of her all through his first year there. Near the end of that year, in the spring, he realised that he was attracted to her. He didn't know what to do. He still felt guilty about his failed marriage with Carol, but he felt vulnerable, too. Underneath all of the rhetoric of their separation, it was clear to him that they were both victims of it. They had committed some outrageous mistakes in their attempt to hold onto their love, and he knew in his heart that Carol had committed at least half of them. She had pushed his passivity beyond its limit and he didn't want that to happen again. Ever. So when he realised that he was being drawn to Sarah he felt uneasy, wary, unsure of himself.

He didn't believe in cliches, nor did he believe in taking advantage of his situation as Sarah's professor. He understood the artificial attraction that occurs so often in that exchange. So he'd stand in the corner at the student dances and watch her dance with her younger friends.

Sarah had a grace about her that he couldn't define. She was a tall, willowy creature. Her hair fell down below her waist and was often braided. She wore funky clothes: loose sweaters over Indian cotton skirts, army boots, bandanas, embroidered shirts. She had a classical, almost Botticelli face that pivoted around the most sensual lips he'd ever seen. The grace rose up from beneath these things, however. She was shy but self-assured. If he asked her a question in class, she'd blush with embarrassment and mumble some inane answer meant to warn him off. But her essays on Vonnegut and Joyce were beyond her age, beyond what they'd been discussing in class. They revealed a perspective that was both sure of itself and excited to be sure of itself. It was wonderful for him to be drawn to her like this. Slowly. It awakened him out of his regrets about Carol and made him feel that he was capable of fun. Of love. Of course, predictably, he wanted to make love to this woman. The thought of her clothes sliding to the floor as her arms reached up for his face made him weak with desire. But even in this, there was a difference: it didn't matter to him when or even if it ever happened. It was all slow in his mind, and he savoured it. There was no frantic motion; it became the one static thing in his life. He just drank her in whenever he could and went about the rest of his life. Then one night, as he leaned against a pillar and listened to the rock band, she came up behind him and asked him if he didn't find it too hot in the hall. He stared back into this innocuous question and offered her his hand and they disappeared out into the spring snow. They walked silently down to the park on the Kootenay Arm and talked all night. He walked her home. That was it. That was the beginning. They didn't make love for half a year. But when they did it meant everything to Peter. He felt that night, as he listened to her sleep, that his chaotic life was reaching out to hold onto something wonderful, something shining that could bless its speed. Direct it forward. Into himself maybe. So when he left Nelson he left it with Sarah's blessing. She was anxious about his drinking, but more about him losing his innocence. She had seen it and guarded it when he couldn't seem to. So his departure was partly their conspiracy. As he snaked across the country in his Datsun, the thought of her carried him forward to face his past. He didn't know if or when he would see her again, but he knew that something had to snap before he could anyway: he didn't want their love to be affected by his past.

Finally, here was Carol opening her apartment door to him in Toronto in September, holding him, confused: not quite knowing him anymore, nor him her. They cried about their past and clutched one another shyly. They had ended something and there was a hesitant peace, even a renewed love in that. They could love each other now because they knew another kind of love was gone. It was over.

Carol's writing had become very disciplined. She was doing well as a free-lancer and had placed four of her short stories in reputable journals. Peter seemed to be whirling in a directly opposed, unhealthy kind of discipline. Carol looked at him and wondered: she could see he'd been living too hard, moving too fast. When she asked him, innocently enough, how he'd found his dad on his trip through Edmonton, Peter answered her literally: he went into a long story about how he'd been standing outside looking through the kitchen window when he'd caught his dad making sandwiches. When Peter described the look on his dad's face when he'd finally glanced up and saw Peter standing there, he couldn't finish his story. He broke down. They were sitting in Mr. Zum's across from Rochdale. Carol watched him and worried about what would happen to him now.

Carol had made a lot of friends in Toronto since Peter left. These were journalists, aspiring writers, women activists. One of the latter had just moved out of a communal house on Shaftesbury Avenue only twenty yards from the Summerhill subway stop. Carol arranged that Peter take her friend's place in the house. The only person still living there was a guy called Bob. On his second day back, Peter went over to talk to him.

It took a long time for Peter and Bob to become friends. It took no time at all, however, for them to realise that they could split the cost of the house, share responsibilities, divide the cooking. Bob had been a lieutenant in the American Army and had deserted in 1968. He'd fled to Toronto and was working on a Ph.D. in American history at York. He was concentrating on the bungling of American foreign policy after the second world war and into the Korean war. He was also the driving force behind an anti-Viet Nam, American-in-exile monthly called *Amex Canada*. There were dangers attached to being the editor of that magazine. The phone was tapped and the house was watched. Bob had become a high-profile voice for the exiles and the FBI kept close track of him. As it turned out, Bob's life was being lived on an edge Peter had never been close to before.

Aside from steady work on his dissertation, Bob spent most of his time on the phone: either long-distance to sympathetic groups in the States, or locally, organising *Amex* issues and soliciting articles. The rest of the time he complained, innocently enough, about the political scene in Canada, and hung out with Marxists of different persuasions, feminists, and other exiles. They would get together and listen to music down at Grossman's or the El Mocambo. Otherwise, Bob's daily schedule was eccentric. He surfaced at noon and went to bed around 4:30 a.m. after sitting in his favorite chair in the living room for hours, reading every line in the five American dailies he'd buy from a news agency down on Yonge. Bob didn't miss a trick.

Bob struck Peter as a fairly lonely person caught up in the political issues circling around him. Like so many others whose lives were shaped by political action, Bob was vulnerable: about not being bigoted, not being too anti-Canadian at a time when our nationalism was dominant, about not being sexist, elitist, etc etc. He suffered that paralysis that sets in when the liberal mind pursues its own logic and it takes a long time to finally act on anything. His vulnerabilities went deeper than that, however. He'd been raised in a small, New England city. His father had been a member of the Army Reserves, an obsessive patriot, and Bob had been reared in a scaled-down version of *Happy Days*. He had been the high-school football and basketball hero. And here he was now, in political exile at the age of thirty, enclosed by all kinds of revolving bitterness. He sat across from Peter and eyed him cautiously over his flimsy Benjamin Franklin glasses. He was dressed down in a calculated way, his balding head balanced by a long, ill-kept pony-tail that fell down his back to his shoulder blades. One night Bob told Peter off-handedly that, yes, both of his parents had died and he'd been unable to cross the line to attend their funerals. He was a lonely person turning in a field of negative passions. In the face of that loneliness Peter was cautious.

That caution was trying at times because Peter disagreed so often with Bob's political analyses, his judgements so arbitrary and final. In a drunken quarrel, Peter could unleash his own sloppy sarcasm and hurt Bob's feelings for weeks. This happened one night when an old friend of Peter's arrived and wanted to meet Bob. Though Sasha was brilliant in some ways, Peter always suspected that her Achilles' heel was a slavish attraction for anything that passed itself off as the "left". The three of them went out to Grossman's. It took no time for Sasha and Bob to align themselves in their causes. They launched into a slowly building crescendo of neo-Marxist-Maoist analyses of the abundant corruptions of the Canadian government and its foolishly shortsighted politicians. Peter sat for a long time nodding quietly in a fringe-like, fellow-traveller agreement. He ordered more and more beer. It was the cowardly approach, he knew, but Sasha and Bob were feeding their ecstasies in the same way. Finally, Peter was unable to sit in silence any longer. He began to unleash a bit of his own bitterness: he'd grown up in much less privileged circumstances than either of them, had carried the usual chip on his shoulder about that ever since; he'd lived in too many parts of the country they were attacking to fall for any kind of "Toronto" solution to things. So he laced their building admiration for one another with shrewd questions, ironic double-talk, what he thought of as cleverly executed sarcasm and innuendo. He was mad at their redemption of the world, couldn't buy it. Afterwards, the disappointment set in, the quiet. Sasha and Bob hadn't expected Peter to ruin such a fine evening with his irrelevant, maudlin attacks. Bob never forgave Peter for that; he eyed him suspiciously whenever they discussed anything political, which was all the time. He typed Peter as a "red-Tory", a prairie anarchist. It all made sense to Bob. But it didn't ruin their friendship, which grew slowly anyway.

Sarah arrived in late September. She brought warmth into their day-to-day lives, something that relieved their serious- ness about everything. Peter had been phoning her regularly since his arrival in Toronto. One night when she admitted that she didn't care for Victoria, didn't think much of the Fine Arts program there, Peter suggested she come and live with him. She'd said yes.

Suddenly he'd found himself standing there, watching the arrival gate, riveted. He saw her before she saw him. There was something about seeing her as she cast her eyes around the terminal for his that intensified how beautiful she looked to him. She was in full bloom. When she finally did catch his eyes, her smile was unselfconsciously sensual. She looked strong, only her eyes betraying a flickering vulnera- bility. This was a major step away from her past and her heart must have been lurching in fear and joy, Peter thought, especially in the face of a future with a person like him. So he stood there awkwardly, self-conscious in his new cordu- roy suit, waiting. This was a fine intersection to begin in, he thought, and he wrapped her up in a fumbling, urgent hug. It will be all right, he thought. And on the drive into down- town Toronto, as they both thought of one another's bodies, they talked calmly about how well things would turn out. He told her about the watercolour courses he'd sought out for her at Three Schools and she became excited. Sarah was a painter. Her work was magical and unpretentious. From the beginning Peter was captivated by it. For years he had been struggling to move beyond the competitive games he'd sensed around himself — the petty one-upmanship that had drained him when he'd first come to Toronto — and Sarah represented an escape from these things. In time she became his anchor, her instincts a gauge by which he could measure honesty in the world. Sometimes Peter wondered whether he might corrupt what he admired in her. So he sat there in the car, watching her out of the corner of his eye, aware of all of her expectations as she grinned beside him into the windshield, of the strength he'd have to muster up to fulfill these and not be a disappointment.

So the three of them, Bob, Peter and Sarah, ended up settling into "the hole". Bob wasn't "into" cleanliness in a big way, but he was paranoid enough about it that it didn't take long to vacuum at least two-hundred pounds of dog hair off every object in the house, fix up the extra room upstairs with broadloom scraps, arrange for the cooking and shopping. It worked out well. Sarah loved Toronto, was lucky with UIC, and took a series of art classes at Three Schools. Peter worked hard on his study of Lowry, and Bob worked away at his parallel obsessions. Bob's daily schedule overlapped theirs and allowed them a good deal of privacy, which they appreciated. The three of them went out for drinks together, a few drives, a picnic or two down to David Balfour, but most of the time each of them was working away intensely with that luminous love one has when one is young and enthralled. Sarah and Peter learned more about one another and drew together, close. Peter luxuriated in their long walks in the park, the late walks down the rainy sidewalks to the Lothian Mews, the subway rides to obscure films, or their evenings of Tom Rush, Eric Anderson or the Good Brothers at the El Mocambo. Some nights they'd just sit at home in the living room and listen to Peter's old Band albums. Peter, Sarah and Bob were living in an idyll, though none of them realised it at the time.

The house whirled in a quiet amalgam of routines. The only serious disagreement occurred one afternoon when Peter returned on the subway from York and found Sarah slumped over the sink in tears. "You've *got* to talk to Bob, Peter. You've *got* to. Look!" Bob had an arrangement with his huge, street-wise dog, Fred. Fred was so old, so lazy and so fat that he lay down to eat. Bob allowed Fred to lick the plates after supper as a concession to these afflictions. He piled

them up for him one by one on the floor and Fred would lie
there, loll his head and floppy ears to the side, and do his
frantic best. What Sarah was pointing at was a sudsy, greasy
sink full of Fred's hair. Though Peter detested scenes, even
small ones, he did draw the line for Bob on that one, and
added additional ultimatums about the regular vacuuming
of Fred's hair everywhere else. Otherwise, the three of them
lived in a warm circle of cautiously growing, inevitably
sealing affections.

In early December, Sarah decided to return to Vernon, her
hometown in B.C. A favorite uncle of hers had become ill and
her mother needed her help. Peter would rejoin her somehow in the spring and finally meet her family. Neither of
them was threatened by the separation. Their relationship,
in some ways, had been forged by mobility and their strength
to survive it, and the result was a constancy that supported
them, together or apart. Though they missed one another,
there was a sureness that held them, that transcended the
distance.

Abruptly, Peter and Bob were alone in the house. Their
days were quiet again, until Richard showed up one afternoon two weeks after Sarah left.

When Peter first arrived at York in 1971 with Carol,
Richard became his closest ally there. Richard had grown up
New York Irish, a Queen's Catholic. He had turned his back
on all that in a rather obvious imitation of the young Joyce,
one of his predictable heroes. Eventually, he'd had to turn
his back on his country, too. He fled the Viet Nam draft in a
spasm of paranoia complicated by an Irish penchant for
revenge that was deep in him. He'd come to Toronto, where
he slipped into the openness that abounded at that time,
especially in Toronto. You could "hang out" and do anything
you wanted as long as you could get a hold of some money
and that seemed relatively easy. You could become a folk-
singer; everyone loved folk-singers. You could become a
poet, a dancer, a potter, or simply pretend to become these

things. You could attend lectures on various forms of meditation and go out afterwards and get absolutely bombed. You could become a vegetarian one day and spend the rest of the week wolfing down hamburgers at Macdonald's. Toronto offered everything and tolerated the most bizarre eccentricities. It was the right landscape for any kind of exile: it had been created for people who wanted to invent a new world. Richard had already completed an M.A. in the States and enrolled at York to complete a Ph.D. His dissertation concerned the significance of the perfect woman, the muse, in the works of Blake, Coleridge, Shelley and Keats. As it turned out this was an appropriate topic for Richard because it represented one side of a serious paradox he lived out in himself. It caused him endless pain and eventually produced the Richard who stumbled into the Shaftesbury house just after Sarah left.

Richard had these two magnificent selves in close competition with one another. He was a brilliant, natural scholar. That part of him, so intent and precise, so full of awe and devotion, was the part he cultivated as a persona he used with women. He courted them with it. Unfortunately, it was also the part that insisted that women fulfill some high expectations. The other part of Richard was an infectious, hilarious, sly and boozing Irish sense of humor which he concealed but which Peter knew well and could easily draw out of him. Richard was a great drinker and a witty conversationalist when drunk. The two of them got into some great times back then, some unforgivable binges. But they were binges that eased the seriousness of the other grad students at York, by-passed the evenings of gossip and whining in the grad student lounge, and instead turned those evenings into fun. The small price paid for this camaraderie was the odd raised eyebrow. The two of them became characters of sorts, but likeable ones, protected by their academic success.

During 1972, Peter's last winter in Toronto with Carol, Richard had fallen in love with and married a young woman from Chicago who wanted to become a music teacher. She played the flute beautifully. She was attracted to Richard for his ambitions, for his eighteenth-century persona of the perfect gentleman, and partly, though less enthusiastically, for his chaotic other side. He was attracted to her innocence, her introspective intelligence, and her close resemblance to the muse figures that obsessed him. For a variety of reasons this coupling seemed doomed from the start. Carol and Peter felt it in their hearts but said nothing, naturally, hoping it would work out. Peter wasn't surprised when Carol wrote to him in Nelson to tell him that Richard and Linda had separated. Peter loved Richard and wrote to him quickly, hoping that the sundering might produce happiness for each of them elsewhere and that their parting hadn't been too harsh, too fraught with that Irish chip on Richard's shoulder. Peter was delighted two years later, when he returned to Toronto and moved in with Bob, to find Richard in great shape, poised perfectly between his selves.

He was living with a sensual, feisty, upper-middle-class woman named Bridgette who was also a student at York. They seemed fiercely attracted to one another, though they fought a lot, mostly about religion. Bridgette had been raised Toronto High-Anglican, and aside from her finely-tuned wit she was still — oddly for these times — very much a part of that way of life. This presented a serious problem to Richard, but not the problem Peter imagined. Richard had assumed the collective belligerence of his Irish forbears and lashed out at the Limey in Bridgette, flailing her with an Irish vengeance that was ruthless at times. What troubled Peter, and he couldn't get an answer out of Richard, was why he would care so much about religion, the relationship being so healthy in other ways, especially sexually. Typical of his buried self, Richard was never one to downplay his sexual achievements. He discussed them in an accumulation of detail that made Peter feel inadequate for days. But the fights went on and eventually the whole affair ended abruptly and cruelly. Though the final battle was complicated by Richard's intensity as he faced the exams for his thesis, Bridgette announced just before Christmas that she was fleeing to England to pursue her studies there, and was considering an engagement to a fellow who was training to be an Anglican priest in London. He was a man whom Richard was aware of in Bridgette's past but whom he assumed she'd discarded for him. After a terrifying farewell, witnessed by an anonymous cab driver and by Bob and Peter through the living room curtains, Richard lurched in tears into their house with a suitcase and a bottle of Scotch, asking them whether they had their usual stock of beer in the hall closet.

The next week was pandemonium. Because Richard was broken, he fed the Irish half with booze. Peter was glad to assist him, an adept with such comfort himself. He tried to cheer Richard up, cracking Irish jokes in ridiculous Irish accents. Bob helped a lot, too, though he regarded Richard's difficulties as a product of his political flight from the States rather than love gone wrong. And so Peter found himself, in the midst of his own confusion, playing Mercutio to Richard's Romeo. They moved Richard and his belongings in with them. They gave him the room which Sarah and Peter had renovated as a den. It was a lot more attractive than Peter's room. One afternoon a week later, when things were calming down, Richard showed up before supper and disappeared up the stairs to his room. Bob and Peter were sitting in the living room, listening to an old album by Martha and the Vandellas, and could hear Richard rattling tissue paper upstairs. Eventually, he emerged before them in an expensive three-piece suit and new brogues. "What d'ye think, lads?" he asked, buoyantly. "What do you expect us to think?" Peter wondered. He heard Richard slip down the stairs early the next morning and thought little of it until he reappeared at noon dressed in that suit carrying a pile of Graham Greene novels under his arm. He ascended the stairs almost ceremoniously. He closed his room from which soon came — considering the long week before and their mutual taste for rock and roll — the overwhelmingly censorious waft of Gregorian Chant music. It hit Peter all at once. Everything fit together suddenly. He realised what he was in for: *Christ!* Richard's transformation was more difficult for Bob to accept than Peter. Peter had grown up Catholic. It had been a familiar environment for him. He had even been in a seminary for a while before his long fall from grace. And that Catholic childhood and especially his family were ever-present in Peter's thoughts anyway. He could never let them go. No matter where he moved or how complicated his life became, he always judged himself from the warmth of the nine of them living together, of the laughter they shared. Watching the spectacle of Richard's sudden retreat reminded him of his own struggle with his father, of their fights and truces, of the drinking at the heart of those negotiations. In his early teens, Peter felt as if he had two fathers: an abstract God whom he talked to but never saw in the life around him, and his real dad lurching through another Saturday night, fuelled and ready to fight. He became so convinced of these two fathers that eventually he decided to become a priest, to nourish the abstract one, make it incarnate by himself. It didn't last long, however, the stillness at St. Joseph's Seminary. Instead, he chose his dad's world, in all its imperfections and heady failures, its excesses and joys. He felt comfortable as he moved through his dad's world, stumbling from one moment to the next, imitating — though he didn't know it then — the design his father had inlaid on the world. In some ways, he sought his own father in everything now. So he could certainly understand how Richard's traumatic double-vision could draw him, especially now, back into the warm, simplistic arms of his Holy Muse, the Church. The early morning Masses down on Bloor or up on St. Clair, that music, the Graham Greene novels, all these walls he could re-erect from memory to enclose the pain. Peter understood what this retreat into ritual offered. For Bob, however, the transformation was awful: an lapse of modern conscience, a snaffling of an original soul back into the seedy clutches of an oppressive, fascist system. The three of them had some dicey arguments, especially when Richard complicated their efforts to console him by going on the wagon for good. Peter missed drinking with Richard and found the house too tense at times. He'd return home from a long day at York, wedge himself past Bob's Maoist analyses of the day's editorial in *The Globe and Mail*, then ascend the stairs with caution, trying not to flush the by-now sanctimonious Richard out of his Gregory the Great trance — his choir of monks, like sirens, drawing Peter back by osmosis into some crazed feudal cathedral for benediction.

Then the spring hit them: a luscious, early spring for Toronto. Flowers budded and the trees fanned out over the tiny green parks that were delicately interlaced through the downtown core. Spring rains fell like silk and you could go for long walks late at night smelling all the fresh green beginnings. Everyone smiled more. The force of this spring defused the rattling triptych back in the house. They began to get along more and more. The pressing issue for Peter was how he was going to be able to raise the cash he needed to drive out west, pick up Sarah, and return for one last summer to Toronto. Luckily, a student of his was working part-time for an Australian guy who owned a small store across the parking lot from the liquor store two blocks away. The store was called The Incredible Mix and it sold every unnecessary thing you'd need to stock a bar: useless little gadgets, glasses, Perrier water, clamato juice, and rows and rows of Schweppe's tonic and soda. It was a cynically attractive little shop run by an even more cynical, ruthless man. He saw pretensions everywhere and capitalised on all of them: sucking every aspiring executive lost in his dream into the perfectly dated cash register which clacked and sang as word of this new place spread throughout the expensive flats taking over this once ancient area of the city.

Brian kept hinting to Peter — before the final grades were submitted — that he might be leaving this part-time job, that his boss just might need a "new man." Peter was thinking more of Sarah than of what he might have to endure in this artificial purgatory, but he made sure that Brian understood that he was willing and able. Finally, Brian took Peter over to meet the man officially. Though he was suspicious when Brian introduced Peter as his "professor" up at York — the owner never having had "no learnin" meself and never fuckin' needed it by Christ!" — he seemed to think that Peter would be suitable and offered him the part-time job at the minumum wage.

Aside from a lot of swipes at the uselessness of educated people, unemployed Ph.D.'s, the virtues of living in *the real world*, the owner turned out to be a tolerable enough human being. Peter could put up with him. He could work for the man. That was his first mistake. Peter was too earnest, tried too hard, and ended up working much harder for this guy than he deserved. The owner quickly spotted this weakness in Peter and, step by step, withdrew from the operation of the store, leaving Peter alone while he spent his afternoons up in his new pool in Thornhill, plotting yet another scam over a neat Scotch. He especially liked to leave Peter with the duties of the afternoon shift, which initiated Peter into the risks of cashing in and locking up. So well was all of Peter's industry working out for him that one morning the owner asked him if he knew another over-educated pal who could use a dose of the real world and split the shifts with him. Peter thought immediately of Richard, who was getting as broke as he was though he didn't show it as much. Eventually, after a similarly insulting interview — which Peter prepared the aristocratic Richard to endure — Richard secured a part-time job, too, and the two of them began to run the business.

In the end Peter never understood just how it happened. He knew that Richard took his books over with him to read in the last few hours of the afternoon shift, and he guessed that Richard might have been more obvious about reading them than he had been. Richard might have been even annoyed by customers interrupting him. It was possible. At any rate the news of this violation somehow reached the ears of their employer. One afternoon when he actually deigned to drop down from Thornhill and Richard had dropped by innocently to purchase a tin of pop on his way home from a late Mass in his three-piece suit, the owner confronted Richard. It began with, "What the fuck d'ya think I'm paying you so much for, to run a fuckin' *library*?" Richard just stood there, shocked by the presumption of this entrepreneur, and in his best combination of a Ford Madox Ford or J.P. Donleavy gentleman, he suggested to Peter that this mutual acquaintance, the owner, could stuff the job up his rectum, that he could *forward* his last cheque to Peter's address, that he'd see Peter later on, wondering, probably, why Peter wasn't throwing a scene, too. Wonder all you want, Peter thought to himself. He disapproved of Richard's eighteenth-century solution, but more honestly, he couldn't afford to be sacked yet. He was still building up the cash he needed for his trip out west.

No matter how hard Peter worked for this man now, no matter how much the owner seemed to like him — even admitting sometimes a small portion of the debt he owed Peter for keeping the operation afloat — a dislike of Ph.D.'s still rattled around in his parsimonious little soul. Peter was having lunch with Carol one Monday, preparing himself for the afternoon shift, when the owner phoned him there — the coward — and told him that business was slowing down, that he didn't need Peter to come in that day. When Peter asked him for the schedule for the next day, the overly-friendly explanation of why that was unneccessary, too, made everything clear to Peter: he was fired. The owner didn't even have the guts to explain it to him face to face. And now that they were both turfed out of the real world, Peter and Richard had some fine talks during which their former boss was hauled through all manner of punishment in Dante's lower circles of hell.

What bothered Peter most about all this afterward was the physical risk, the very real fear he had endured. The liquor store across the parking lot was located in the abandoned CPR Station, but it remained one of the most notorious outlets in Toronto — mostly because of its closeness to Yonge, Bloor and the subway. Though the neighborhood around it had been transforming into an "in" place to live, this old liquor store was still haunted by hordes of the real losers in this city, the drifters. They used the liquor store as their base for operations. They slept in David Balfour Park, three blocks away, in the spring and summer, and in flop-houses or the Sally-Anne down on Jarvis when winter hit. The Incredible Mix seemed a natural target for their contempt and cunning nose for cash. It was the perfect opportunity, it seemed to Peter, for being rolled in that area, especially at 11:00 p.m. when it was obvious — the store's front windows a flourescent invitation to anyone on the make — that Peter was emptying the cash from the till, rolling and marking it, and taking it into the back room to lock it up in the safe. While Peter was working there two young men had been murdered tending Becker's Milk Stores in the same general area. From Peter's point of view, The Incredible Mix was a much more lucrative and even more justifiable target.

Peter began to get nervous, even frightened sometimes, never having had to experience that kind of fear before in any other city. What bothered him most, aside from the increasingly imagined possibility of being rolled or even murdered, was that he was putting his life on the line for this successful operation which he objected to in principle anyway. The last straw occured at 10:50 p.m. one night a week before he was fired. Peter noticed, in his accumulating paranoia about these things, that a battered 1968 Chevy with two guys in it had been sitting out in the parking lot between the two stores for about three hours. When Peter switched off the power to the neon and began fumbling in the till, he saw the car's lights flash on suddenly, then off again. Twice. He was sure it was a signal. Peter imagined that this was it: a sordid, ridiculous martyrdom in the cause of some sleazy capitalism, his employer shaking his head sadly for the news cameras the next morning. Peter's heart was pounding, and fantasies played themselves out like options of scenes in movies like *Taxi Driver*. Somehow he managed to get the wad of cash into the back room, lock the safe, switch off the interior lights one by one — his ears antennae for guns and knives, for footseps — and proceed to lock up the front door to the store from the outside. This was his greatest moment of panic. He figured that it was the perfect moment for *them*, his fingers rattling, trying to get those two locks to tumble and release the keys.

He bounded across the parking lot to the paradise of the liquor store, bought a mickey of rye, and walked over to their house never so glad to see Richard and Bob sitting around the kitchen table fighting. Peter sat there with the two of them and got drunk: slowly, methodically, his fear shifting into self-mockery. He was only partly aware of the argument Richard and Bob were having about the value of the human soul on the one hand, its spirit and dignity, and the real, concrete virtues of the Chinese commune on the other. Peter was ecstatic to exchange The Incredible Mix for this one: exchange a tawdry death for two Americans fighting over the twentieth century.

Two nights later he sat up through the night in his tiny red room, reading and staring out the window. He was enthralled by the fear that had gripped him that night at The Incredible Mix. He wondered what he thought he was trying to do with his life, why he was pushing himself so hard to turn his back on his beginnings, to survive in this new territory he had claimed as his future. He wondered if one could be vigilant in a landscape that was less chaotic. In time, the sun turned his former, dark, imagined feast of worms into some contemporary pastoral: people walking singly and in groups, smiling, with or without umbrellas, grinning their ways downward into the subway entrance. He knew

absolutely then that he wanted out. He wanted a way back.
Peter wanted highways, grain elevators nine miles apart,
mountains, Sarah. The next afternoon he received an offer of
a teaching job at the University of Regina.

Peter sees the two of them in his rear-view mirror waving
goodbye. His last glimpse of the house and these two men
becomes a concretion of their times, the word made flesh and
alive: a world to be improved upon but never regained. As
in a dream, they are all out on an edge in this memory,
wavering between the worlds they have fashioned for themselves and which have been fashioned for them. There are
gardens everywhere, it seems. Richard is standing erect in
his three-piece suit ready for Mass; Bob is leaning, one hand
on the doorframe, his newspaper swaying from the other.
The headlines read AMNESTY A REAL POSSIBILITY. The
Datsun pulls away onto the asphalt, leaves Toronto as a
Canaletto haze in its rear-view mirror, the windshield promising, promising.

Hangovers

So, I'm goin down the road, boys.
I'm seekin what I'm owed, boys.
And I guess it must get better
If far enough I go.
- Nova Scotia Ballad

1.

Ever since Uncle Fred decided to go back to Nova Scotia for a visit he'd been more and more anxious. That was understandable enough though it seemed disproportionate to his age and the many other times he'd made the trip. We decided there was something special about this one. There was something else on his mind.

I arrived in Edmonton for a short visit on my way back to Regina. It was two weeks before Uncle Fred was scheduled to leave, and I could see what was happening to him. He had relied on my mother, Helen. Rely is not good enough. Though my mother would chuckle about it, she understood the responsibilities she'd been drawn into. Uncle Fred knew from experience, as we all knew, that my mother was a professional organizer. Though we kidded her mercilessly • about this if it were late at night and we'd been partying, Uncle Fred never kidded her and never had. He was in awe of her. He appreciated what she could do for him: in the long run, everything. She reserved him an economy-fare ticket months in advance; she bought him some new luggage; she calmed him down about the wait and switch of planes in Toronto. Everything you need to arrange or think about in this kind of situation, my mother had already done. The

funny thing was that even though Uncle Fred knew that in
our mother's hands he was as good as in Nova Scotia already,
that didn't seem to ease his worrying.

Uncle Fred would phone my parents every day about
some small detail he'd forgotten to discuss. Though Dad
would mock him—laughing his laugh into the phone so that
we'd know who he was talking to — both my parents more
than tolerated Fred's anxiety. This was because they liked
him. It was also because his fastidiousness had become a part
of what they lived with now, with most of us gone, and
especially since Fred himself had gone on the wagon. They
certainly preferred his new way to his old.

Uncle Fred had always phoned my parents when he lived
up north. His phone-calls had been ritual, a part of how we
ordered our years. They came in a pre-ordained sequence
that had the same effect as major weather changes. Looking
back on them, they followed that other, natural cycle closely:
in the fall, around his birthday; just before Christmas to tell
us he was coming down to stay for the holiday; at Easter
when he was lonely, and finally, late in June to acquaint us
with his summer plans, plans that inevitably revealed that
he was coming to stay with us. After he had moved to
Edmonton for good, he'd phone late at night from a hotel
downtown — usually The Mayfair or The Cecil — where he
was loaded and in some kind of a fix. His calls were always
dramatic. It's just that since he'd quit drinking they were
more happy dramas.

But we still smiled automatically when we heard Uncle
Fred's voice on the other end of the line. You can't ignore a
gift like his easily. My dad and I were always convinced that
a comedian like Bob Newhart could have made millions if
we'd taped Fred's calls. Though I wasn't there when it happened, my parents did tape him one Christmas. As always,
they phoned my dad's mother in New Glasgow to wish her
a merry Christmas. Uncle Fred happened to be there at the
time — in his way — and eventually, after a good deal of

nervous warnings from my mother, they put him on the line. Fred was bombed and feeling sentimental, ambiguously sentimental, about talking to 'mama':

"Mama?"

"Phillip?"

"Mama?"

". . . is that *you*. . . *Fred*?"

"Who the hell did ya tink it was?" You can hear Uncle Fred laughing mysteriously now.

"Is that *you* . . . *Fred*?"

"Mama!"

"Well. How *nice*. How're you makin out boy?"

"Not . . . too. . .bad. . .*by!*" There is a long, melodramatic pause. "Thanksforthesweatermama."

"Oh, you *got* it, then?"

"*Shore* I did!"

"Well how does it *fit*?"

"Not. . .too. . .*good*. . .by!"

"Not too good? Come on with you now." Nana laughs highly, lightly. "Was it too *big* Fred?"

"S'too damn *small* fer Chrissake!" Laughter from both of them. Another long pause. "Mama? Howoldsareyounowanyways?"

"I'm forty-eight. . ."

"You're *what*?"

"I'm eighty-eight now. *You* know that, Fred."

Another long pause. You can detect a few muffled sobs from Fred. "I thought you said you were *forty*-eight fer Chrissake. *I'm* forty-nine!"

"Oh, Fred!"

Long pause. "My god but you're a mmmwunnerful mrother!"

"Well, how's *Beverly* doing Fred?"

"Oh she *left* me about three months ago."

"She *did*?"

"*Shore* she did."

"Oh. . . well why'd she do *that*?"

"Mama?"

"Yes?"

"You didn't get a card from me. That's fer *shore!*"

"Oh Fred, *that's* all right."

"Youdontunderstand."

"You don't have to send me. . ."

"I would have sent you. . . a Christmas card. . ."

"Yes?"

"But I didn't. . . have the *money*. . . to *buy*. . . the *stamp!*" Fred is breaking down now, his voice trailing off at its highest pitch.

"Oh Fred, boy!"

"Ah, ta *hell* with ya."

"Hi mama? It's Helen again."

2.

I don't like hangovers, but I usually know how to get rid of them in advance. Because Sarah and I stayed at my brother's house, I had forgotten about my ritual 222s and when Blanche called up the stairs at noon I was in the middle of a bad one. I met Blanche half-way down the stairs. "It's your Uncle Fred," she said. Terrific.

"Hi, Uncle Fred."

"*Peter!* How're you doin?"

"Pretty good."

"Were you *asleep*, boy?"

"I was just getting up anyway."

"Say, *Peter*?"

"Right?"

Uncle Fred's voice softens into a whisper. "Do you want to do your dad a favour boy?"

"Right."

Loud again. "You see, Peter. . .your father's over here."

"Yes?"

Soft again. "Well. . . let's *face* it boy. . . he's *loaded!*"

"Right."

Loud again. "And he has to go pick up the car by one o'clock."

"Right."

Soft to loud. "Helen'll give him *shit*, boy, if he doesn't come through. She'll be cheesed off to the *nines!*"

"I'll be over right away."

"You're going to come over then?"

"Yeah, I'll be over in about twenty minutes."

"She'll *kill* him!"

"Don't worry about it Uncle Fred."

"OK boy. I'll put on a *coffee*."

"Right. That's great."

"It's *instant*."

"That's OK."

"I don't have a perculator."

"No problem."

"OK?"

"Right. See you soon Uncle Fred."

"OK boy."

"Bye."

"*Roger!*"

3.

I was seven the morning I first met Uncle Fred. It was a
Saturday at the end of the month or just after the baby-cheque
arrived because Mom had told us the night before that we'd
get our allowance in the morning. It was a big day. We'd all
get a quarter, and Evelyn and Richard and I would walk
down to Gould's Drugs and spend it. We were excited when
we got up early. Saturday mornings and that walk to the
drug store. We were all in pajamas when he knocked on the
door.

Mom and Dad had talked to us often about Uncle Fred
and all our other relatives we'd never met or couldn't remember meeting. My parents had moved to Edmonton with the
three of us in the summer of 1952, all the way from Antigonish by train. I think we remembered more about the trip itself
than those few years before it. The move must have been a
wrenching one for them because they'd left everyone and
everything behind them, for the future, for us I guess. That's
why they talked so much about relatives. At the time, of
course, we couldn't understand either their pain or their
interest in all these mythical people. The names they laughed
about late at night. We simply accepted all this new Edmonton and neighborhood and sunlit fantasies about the school
two blocks away as a matter of course, as children do. All we
could guess about Uncle Fred was that he must have been
especially funny because his was the name that made them
laugh most. Children look forward to funny people, but we
weren't ready for Uncle Fred standing there at the door,
falling into our mother's arms in his Navy uniform, a myth
become three-dimensional. Moving. Something you touch
with awe. The first of these names to really *be*.

To be, and be shrewd too. Uncle Fred's first laughing and hooting act, after he'd kissed my Mom and pumped Dad's hand, was to waltz all of us down to Gould's Drugs by himself. There he announced in an overly-loud voice to Mr. Gould — who we'd always thought of as odd in his primness — "By the jeez, I want a *quart* of ice-cream for *shore*! And these three kids here can have *anything* they *want*! That's *another* for shore."

"I see."

"I'm Phillip Bendy's *brother*. . . he's my *brother*, by!"

"Oh, I. . ."

"Just got in this marnin from goddamn *Toronto*. By *train*, by!"

"Yes?"

"Of course, I'm *loaded*!"

"Well, I. . ."

"He's my *brother*, buddy, and *don't*. . . *you*. . . *forget* it!"

"*Look* Mr. Bendy. . ."

"Don't you *look me*! I'm from Nova *Scotia*. From *Westville*!"

"That well may be, but I. . ."

"And these are my *relatives*!"

"You've made that quite. . ."

"*Drive 'er juke, there's herrin in the by!*"

Uncle Fred lived with us for three years before going north to Fort Chipewyan to teach at the Indian school there among all those priests and nuns. Memories of him divide into two distinct lines: the specific things that happened while he was with us day to day, and the phone calls and visits we'd get from him when he was up north.

The routine business was difficult for us at first. When we saw him during the day Uncle Fred always seemed so serious, meticulous, even cranky about us helping out Mom and

Dad more. We referred to this side of him as his Michael B.
Anthony side: the Mr. Manners we'd come to know so well
on TV. That was only one side, however. The other emerged
late at night, on weekends particularly, and especially on
those nights when he was supposed to be babysitting us. On
those nights this other side was more like us. Uncle Fred
would turn into a kid again, play games with us, tell us that
Mom and Dad could go to hell for all he cared, and
eventually, almost always, he'd get sentimental about Nova
Scotia and finally pass out on the couch, or worse — and this
would cause more trouble with Mom later on — he'd start
phoning long-distance to Nova Scotia. Evelyn, Richard and
I came to know very early the cause of this transformation,
and I think we babysat him a lot, too. I remember two
incidents. Uncle Fred lying on the couch sobbing for Nova
Scotia with his nose running. We had to lug him to bed so
that Mom and Dad wouldn't catch him. It was the runny nose
that bothered us the most. Another image: Uncle Fred sitting
for what seemed three days solid one summer in the red chair
in the kitchen, his head down on his chest only bobbing up
now and then to sob, "He's my brother!" every hour or so, or
alternately, and with a loud sarcastic laugh, "I'm OK at *The
Bay*, by!" This was a reference to his bad credit at the Hudson
Bay Store downtown, a monolith which Uncle Fred considered his enemy, everything he stood against. "They don't
treat you like that in Nova Scotia, by the jeez," he'd shout.
"Not in the Navy neither."

The phone calls from the north were another matter,
something we had to interpret from Mom and Dad's com-
ments. Mom filled us in about Uncle Fred's job up north.
Because she loves facts and details, she was as obsessed with
where he was as we were. And since Dad was a teacher we
didn't have any trouble imagining what Fred did; we just
wondered how he managed those two sides with all those
priests and nuns for company, and without us to look after
him. The organised, fastidious side of him arrived peri-
odically in meticulously packaged bundles of snapshots of

smiling Indian children, serious-looking weathered priests and nuns, husky dogs and lots of snow. The other side arrived at Christmas and Easter and, often, for the whole summer. Uncle Fred usually whooped into the house unexpectedly with a rousing "Driver McIver!" and left, either weeks or months later, in tears, loaded, Mom and Dad packing him into a Cessna. "I don't want to go, by!" he'd sob to Dad, "I'm so friggin lonely up there." They'd always get him on the plane, though there were a few close calls. Soon, within weeks, his organised side would arrive in the mail again. We were, of course, getting older and wiser all this time, and began to understand these melodramas in more complicated ways: we wondered more, privately, why people did these things to themselves again and again.

4.

There is something I have to describe before the door opens here, but it's difficult to put into words: my father's laugh these days. Over all the years I have watched him, including those years when he began to drink more and more, my father taught me what cynicism and sarcasm mean when they're real: when you hear them and recognise the truths they speak. That doesn't mean that my father is a hard or a cold person. As he admits frequently, he is really sentimental. He'll confess this as an apology. What his laugh contains these days is some intricate mixture of all of these contradictory emotions. It begins as a bottled fart forcing itself slowly through a pin-hole in an old whoopee cushion, and eventually breaks out into loud, wheezing rasps. When he's been drinking this noise is his way of punctuating a view of the universe which combines tremendous scorn for human pretension, and a deep and sensitive gratitude that these pretensions exist so he can laugh at them. The smallest crime can get this epic machinery going. My way of indicating this spasm is to write "Blaphat!" But you really *do* have to *be* there to appreciate the fullness of it, especially if it's aimed at you.

5.

"*Peter*, boy, how're you doing?"

"Great, Uncle Fred."

My father's head swooped up from the table to focus on my entrance. "Blaphat!"

"Oh, Phillip! Come on now!"

"Hi Dad."

"Blaphat!"

"Come *on* Phillip!" My uncle was grinning, taking my father in. His stare was a curious mixture of solicitousness, admiration and glee. He'd always looked up to this older brother, and since he'd quit drinking Uncle Fred's affection for Dad had increased. His old, boisterous dependence on Dad had turned, not away from dependence exactly, but towards a mixture of it and a mushrooming sense of care. He'd do things for my father. His "Mr. Manners" side had taken over after he'd quit the booze and at fifty-three he was suddenly drawn to gestures: giving gifts, writing people, lending my Dad the money for a mickey, going down home to see his mother, fixing up his apartment so that it looked just right. Fixing up his apartment had become his greatest obsession. Possibly it was the simple need to build a home for himself after all those years of having none, of moving around.

"Your father's a *case*, boy!"

"Blaphat!"

"Go on over there and sit down, Peter, and I'll put on the water for a coffee."

"That would be great, Uncle Fred."

"Blaphat!"

"It's *instant*, boy."

"No problem. I like instant."

"Blaphat!"

Uncle Fred laughed at himself and began to putter about his small kitchen: filling the kettle with water, placing a cup out on the counter with a small spoon beside it, bringing out a jar of Taster's Choice from another cupboard. While he wiped the counter off with a damp J-Cloth, he asked me if I'd eaten anything. I told him I had and that all I really wanted was a good cup of coffee. I glanced around the apartment and noticed that Uncle Fred had been filling it up since I'd first seen it in the spring. Dad's head bobbed up to screen Fred's apartment as if for the first time. "Yes. It's certainly looking great now," he said. "Did you show Peter the TV?"

Uncle Fred walked over to an old mahogany console. "Look at *this*, Peter. I shore got a good deal on this." I got up and went over to examine the set with him. It was one of those old combination TV, radio and record players from the late fifties. It was in good shape. Fred patted it and smiled at me proudly, "Fifty skins if you can believe that, boy!" At the word skins my dad convulsed again and Fred laughed, too. "Of course, your *father* there had to come and *get* it for me. In his *car*. Which was quite an *occasion!*"

"I bet."

"I'm always asking him to drive me around."

"That's all right," Dad remarked seriously, "You *did* get a good deal on it."

"You sure did. How does the stereo work?"

"You won't believe it, boy." Uncle Fred opened the cabinet and put on one of his favorite Waylon Jennings albums. This music made Dad laugh.

"It sure works great," I said.

"Shore it does."

"Of *course* it does," my father insisted. "You got a real good deal on that one. *Period.*"

The water was boiling now, so Fred went over to fix my coffee and I sat down across from Dad again. I looked over at Fred moving meticulously around his small kitchen to the tune "I Don't Think Hank Done It This-A-Way." He brought the coffee over and sat to my right, the three of us like a perfect triangle inscribing the circumference of a circle in the corner of his kitchen. I slouched over my coffee and the ashtray. Dad leaned back into his grins, one hand flat on the table, the other folded almost ceremoniously over a raised knee that flexed over the other leg as he listened and talked. Fred sat very straight, almost rigid in his chair, dressed in black, wearing what I would call army boots polished black. Part of his new uniform, I guessed. Whenever he'd look over at Dad Uncle Fred would grin that half-smile of his that reminded me of his Cape Breton jokes and stories. He was doing this now. "Well, your *father's* got to pick up his car by one o'clock."

"I *know* that *Fred*."

"Right," I said.

"I *know* you *know*, Phillip, for Christ's sake," Fred laughed. "But that's why Peter's here."

"*I* can pick up the car *myself*, Fred. What are you *talking* about? Don't you worry about *that*, boy."

"Dad, you're so loaded right now, you couldn't get out the *door*."

"RRRRrrrriiiigggghhhhttt!" Dad laughed, then tried to look very serious. "I'm all right. Don't you worry about *that*. *Period*."

"Right."

"RRRRrrrriiiigggghhhhttt!"

"So, I guess you're ready for the flight home, eh?" I asked Uncle Fred.

"Blaphat!"

"Yes, I am. Of course your mother and father there have figured it all out to a *tee!*"

"That should be great. How long do you go for?"

"I've got three weeks off. But I won't stay the full three. Just two. Then I'll have a week off here before I go back to work. A week off here."

"It'll be great for Nana," I said.

"Certainly it will," Dad said.

"Well, at any rate, *I'm* looking forward to it. And I've still got a few things I've got to get organised."

"Blaphat!"

"But your mother's taking care of all that," and Fred laughed, too.

"Right."

"I just don't like *planes*, boy."

"Blaphat!"

"What are you laughing at?" I asked Dad. "You weren't exactly tap-dancing your way off that flight to Vancouver."

"All *right. I* know. But I'm a pro now. A jet-setter now."

"Right."

"RRRRrrrriiiigggghhhhtttt."

"And your apartment looks great," I said to Fred.

He glanced around his new home. "I'm filling it up bit by bit you understand. Thing's are getting into shape, you know. I've got a raise coming up soon, and things are looking pretty good, boy." He winked at me.

"Did you finish all that stuff with Beverly and the lawyers?" I asked him.

"Sure he did," Dad said, seriously.

"Oh. I *shore* did!" Fred said. "No. That's all settled now. I mean, there weren't any problems you understand. I guess it was pretty clear. She's been *shacked up* with that other guy for over a year now."

"Right."

"Blaphat!"

"I mean, I can *take* that, boy. It's just that I get so cheesed off when she phones for money. He's a trucker for Christ's sake. Makes more money that I ever will. With that inheritance coming in and all I didn't want any trouble, boy, I can tell you that for shore!"

"Well, it's good it's settled anyway," I said.

"Right," Dad offered.

"And it's not that I don't see her occasionally you understand. We get along OK. It's just that when she phones me up in the middle of the night, boy, asking for money, I get cheesed off to the *nines*."

"Blaphat!"

"Right."

"RRRRrrrriiigggghhhhhtttt!"

"But we still talk. I meet her downtown sometimes." The thought of Uncle Fred and Beverly meeting for coffee down at The Bay reminded me of Carol and me getting together since we'd separated.

"Did you see my *bed*, Peter?"

"You mean that couch over there?"

"Blaphat!"

Uncle Fred laughed. "I *thought* you'd guess." He got up and walked over to the couch. "No. Your *mother* figured this one out for me."

"Blaphat!"

"As per usual." Fred pulled the seat forward to reaveal the tidily made bed concealed beneath it.

"That's really handy," I said.

"It shore is." Fred returned to his chair. "*You* know. You don't want to have people coming over and your bed's right there before their *eyeballs* for Christ's sake!"

"Blaphat!"

"Right."

"RRRRrrrriiiigggghhhhtttt!"

"No. You know what I mean Peter. And Helen found a real good deal on it, too. At *Woodward's*."

"You sure it wasn't MacDonald's Fred?" Dad suggested.

Fred laughed. "They do it all for me, by."

"Blaphat!"

"No. I've been getting the place fixed up. It's looking fair to middlin'."

"Right."

"RRRRrrrriiiigggghhhhtttt!"

Fred winked at me. "All I need now is a *woman* for Christ's sake!"

Dad almost slipped off his chair he was laughing so hard. We all were. Aside from it being funny and brilliantly timed, that had been a strange thing for my uncle to say. None of us really talked openly about these things. We'd all wondered about Fred's loneliness after Beverly, but had never mentioned it.

"Oh Fred," Dad said. "You're going to make out OK, boy."

"I *know* that, Phillip," Fred said and winked at me again.

"Well, you *are*, boy. And don't you forget it. *Period*."

"I know, Phillip, I know. If you only knew the half of it though."

"What do you mean?" Dad shouted.

"Well, I haven't exactly been sitting on me *arse* as far as all that's concerned you know."

"As far as *what's* concerned?" Dad laughed out, exasperated.

Fred laughed over at me and shook his head. "Boy, the trouble I've gotten into."

"What do you mean, Uncle Fred?"

"Blaphat!"

Fred lit up a cigarette, took a long coy drag, and talked through his Cape Breton grin. Winking and chuckling as much to himself as to us. "Well, first off I looked in the paper and heard about . . . you know . . . those singles dances."

"Blaphat!"

"Well, what would *you* do for Christ's sake?"

"Well I. . ." fumbled Dad.

"Anyways. I checked it out. I'm not *stupid* you know. I checked it out with this guy I work with."

"Not Arnje?" Dad shouted.

"Certainly. Arnje. I checked it out with him."

"Blaphat!"

"And I found out where it was. You know. One of those ballrooms down by the goddamn Bay."

"I think I know which one you mean," I said.

"Anyways. I even went down there one night . . . and *almost* went in."

"Blaphat!"

"*Shore* I did! You'd better believe it."

"What happened?" I asked.

Fred took another long, playful drag while Dad twittered, anticipating the end of Fred's story. Then Fred started laughing, too. "I took *one* look in the door and realised I'd have to be absolutely *loaded* just to get *in* there for Christ's sake! So I went home, naturally. *Period.*"

"Blaphat!"

"But that's not the end of it."

"What do you *mean*, Fred?" Dad shouted again.

"Well, I wasn't going to give up *that* easily."

"*What* do you *mean?*" Dad was really enjoying this.

"I phoned one of those companies."

"Blaphat!"

"You mean computer dating?" I asked.

"*Certainly!*" Fred proclaimed, mocking himself. "I talked to this guy, told him my age and everything. It was as bad as applying for unemployment."

"Yes?"

"YYYYYYyyyyyeeeessss?"

"Well, I had to take in a photograph and *everything* for Christ's sake! And the guy looked me straight in the eye and asked me if I was serious."

"Blaphat!"

"Well, I told him *certainly* I am! And I *was*, too!"

"Yes?"

"YYYYYYyyyyyeeeessss?"

"Well. He phoned me up one night and told me that he'd arranged this meeting for me on such and such a day at such and such a time."

"Yes?"

"Well?"

"*Well, I didn't show up, of course!*"

"Blaphat!"

"What happened then?" I asked him.

"I couldn't make it, boy," Fred laughed to me. "I couldn't go into some stupid room and talk to some woman I'd never met before!"

"And?"

"Well of course — there's always an of course — the guy himself phones me the night afterward. Renege they call it. And boy was he cheesed off!"

"Blaphat!"

"Really?"

"Oh, certainly. He told me he'd never talk to me again. That I'd led him and his clients on. That he never wanted to see my *miserable* face again in his life!"

Though we were all laughing at this, I noticed Dad's laughter was modified. He said suddenly, seriously, to his open palm, "Don't you worry about *that*, Fred. You're going to make out OK. *Period*."

"I *know* that, Phillip," Fred answered him, still laughing. "I've got all sorts of things planned. I've got connections."

"Blaphat!"

Fred looked over at me and winked slyly. "No. I'll tell you a secret, boy."

"Yes?"

"My trip back home?"

"Right?"

"*What* are you getting at Fred?" Dad shouted.

"Give me a chance will you Phillip?" Again, Fred lit up a cigarette, his story already altering his face into chuckles and crowsfeet. "You don't have a *clue* about what I've been up to, Phillip."

"Blaphat!"

"What's up, Uncle Fred?"

"I've got connections. Contacts. In New Glasgow. Don't you worry boy."

"*In New Glasgow?*" Dad was completely exasperated now.

"*Shore*, in *New Glasgow*. I've got contacts, boy."

"What the hell are you planning Fred?"

"Right."

"RRRRrrrriiiigggghhhhtttt!"

"Well, I might be meeting up with an old friend while I'm there."

"Get to the *point*, Fred. You don't really think . . . "

"I don't *think*, Phillip. I *know*. I've already set things up." Fred laughed. "That's why I'm so *nervous* for Christ's sake."

"You don't mean . . ."

"*Shore* I do! *Who else? Elaine McIvor!*"

"But *Fred*! She's married!"

"She certainly *isn't*."

"Blaphat!"

Fred winked at me. "Not anymores anyways."

"What do you mean, Fred?" Dad shouted.

"I *mean* she's been separated for years! A few anyways."

"Who told you that, Fred?"

"Wouldn't *you* like to know for Christ's sake! I *told* you. I've got *contacts*. Through Elsa." Fred was referring to their older sister, Elsa, who lives in New Glasgow.

"That's great, Uncle Fred."

"Blaphat!"

"Well, *you* know what I mean, boy. I doubt I'll ever see her."

"Blaphat!"

"But you never know. I've got contacts."

"Have you asked *her* about all of this?" Dad asked.

"Certainly *not*."

"Jesus, Fred. Elaine McIvor."

Fred went on to explain to me who she was while Dad laughed disbelief throughout. She and Fred had almost been engaged just before the war. She'd lived in Pictou and he'd visited her often. He had given her a ring that her parents knew nothing about. Then the war had come and after Dad

enlisted in the army, Fred had eventually lied about his age
and had been accepted into the Navy. He didn't tell me what
had happened when he returned home from the war. I
suspect that she'd already married someone else. Fred enlisted again and, eventually, after serving a few more years,
he'd ended up at our house with his duffle bag on that
morning in 1954. "Anyways," Fred concluded, "I can't waste
too much time thinking about all *that*. She's likely as big as a
house anyways."

"Blaphat!"

"No. I can't think about that all that much," Fred laughed
to Dad. "I'm too busy *working* for Christ's sake."

It was time to go, but before we left Uncle Fred wanted to
show me something. He disappeared into his hall closet and
reappeared, magically, in his new uniform. It had been re-
cently issued to the Veteran's Affairs Commissionaires. It
looked sharp, even jaunty on him. That and his guileless
smile made him look younger. He announced that his boss
was from Nova Scotia, too. From Halifax. He had served in
the war, too, as a Sergeant Major and had done police work
until he retired. Fred said this guy was as hard as nails but
had a soft, Islander's heart underneath. "Do you think she'll
like it?" he asked, proud of himself.

And so he appeared before me again, a young soldier
from the Maritimes. All the years in between faded as he
stood there, hungover from a binge someone else had thrown
that he couldn't find his way home from. And I could hear
my Dad wheezing behind me, caught between laughter and
sobs. Though he wore a different uniform and had created a
home somewhere else, he was still out there somewhere, too,
caught. And who threw these binges, I wondered. Who
claimed these people and then left them later, stranded,
fumbling. These lives. It wasn't fair, I decided, and wondered
vaguely about my uniform, my war, my home. This binge.
Here.

6.

I returned to the southside by descending into the valley and crossing the Groat Bridge. I should have come that way in the first place; it's always faster. On our descent Dad kept laughing a lot. He got a kick out of the fact that I was always moving around, my small car packed with all our belongings, this time for Regina. He'd glance in the back every now and then when he wanted to let loose. He said, finally, seriously, "Don't you worry about old Fred, boy. He'll make out all right."

"I know he will, too, Dad."

"Blaphat!" As Dad looked out his window, I thought again of Uncle Fred.

He and I were alone in the house on a Saturday night. It was before we had a TV, so I must have been eight. His first year there. We'd listened to Foster Hewitt on the radio, but that was over now. Everyone else was in bed. I know now that Uncle Fred must have been loaded, but I didn't know that then. We had a bow and arrow set: one of those cheap sets for children which included eight plastic arrows with suction cups. Though I forget what we'd been talking about, I remember both of us firing arrows into a watercolour painting in my parent's dining room. It was a typical painting of a Nova Scotia inlet: small, crumbling cabins and piers, a vast and green rambling landscape behind these, and two or three sailboats tied, listing in a small bay. There is no wind in the painting, and the sun shines exquisitely and blasts the sky. Uncle Fred was shooting arrows into all of that, repeating in a fierce whisper, "Kiss me arse!" His laughter accelerated with each loud, vulgar smack of the arrows on the glass as if he were erasing some pretentious but wonderful past he had dreamed as a future for himself, and which, even if it had been true for him for a time — his pastoral — had since been fixed there before him as an object of scorn. "Kiss me arse!"

Dad asked me what I was going to do that afternoon. I told him that I was going over to visit Jesse, Kristyn and Heather, my nephew and nieces, my brother Richard's children.

"Blaphat!"

Dad was looking out his window at the groomed and manicured Mayfair Golf and Country Club. I watched him as his laugh exploded at that artificial paradise, and I laughed at it, too. Suddenly, through the corner of my eye, I saw his head bob up furtively to take me in. After his laugh had shredded the silence I looked over at him just long enough to catch something different twisting on his face. Then I heard him ask the glove compartment, "Do they call you *Uncle* Peter yet?"

"No. They call me Peter."

"Blaphat!"

And we both began to laugh his laugh deeply, my imitations pushing him to more ingenious variations as the car rounded through the traffic circle at the crest of the hill and approached the service station.

The Screen

He is alone. Finally. After all of his whining, his indirect complaints and confused resistance to their fun, his regaling of their too-much-time-together for more openings, more time for himself, for his work, alone. Finally, after all of his oblique masques of edginess, Peter sits alone at the table, having closed and locked the apartment door. He stares at his neatly arranged piles of papers and books. He is finding his hologram wanting.

He is bored.

Peter runs his hand through his dark brown hair and catches the surface of the ceiling above him. That cheap stuff they spray on gyproc, he sighs. Artificial ceiling, and he grins. The point is to simply *suggest* a ceiling. That's it. You merely build tricks for the eye — not the body — to construct the world now. You create the illusion of solids, sell satisfaction *that* way. Like so many things around us now, he thinks, we have actually trained ourselves to stop at the surfaces of things. And not just at the static surface of a ceiling or rug, the cheap metal on a car, or the surface of an actual situation or the look on a person's face, but the whole movie of all these things in motion. We have trained our consciousness to be a lens which is only dissatisfied when the kinetic surfaces stop and you have to focus suddenly, or worse, when those surfaces stop so obviously that their great imperfect under-structure of boredom terrifies. He almost writes this down, it sounds so good. He does write it down. He might use it later in a poem. At least after writing it down he feels as if he is doing what he fantasized he'd do when he was alone. When he'd achieved that surface.

But I know what it's worth, he sighs, and stares at the phone instead.

Yes, it's a nice phone. White. A white wall phone. And he remembers that time in Toronto. The salesperson at Bell had tricked him. She'd asked him if he wanted a coloured phone. "No, I don't want a colour phone. Just the ordinary kind." Clever, clever. "You want a white phone, then?" "Yes, yes, a white phone, sure." Which he got. What he hadn't realised, naturally, was that only the colour black was considered no colour. So he began to pay for a coloured phone all year. And it was only white. Is it white or black that contains all the colours, he wonders, his hand slipping across the arborite photograph of walnut to reach for a cigarette. Which is the one that shuts them all out?

He can't remember.

I'm such a sucker for phones anyway, he thinks. The money I've spent, and eventually owed, in Toronto, in Nelson, in Regina. And here in Vernon. How did all that happen? All that reaching out, me at my most sincere and artificial selves simultaneously, distanced ears interpreting those surfaces. Me with my long list of news beside me so I'd never forget anything. Vulnerable, audacious entreaties. I seem always to be extending this self here out to some soft voice on the other end of the line, me promising a future, the voices always believing me. Not believing me always. That's something, he thinks. All those calls. Thousands of dollars' worth. Usually made late at night, too, courtesy of beer or Scotch. And a plummeting, fearful heart. Usually with my mind on a body, too. Reaching out of here for somebody's flesh. A kind of maudlin, sweet contradiction in that, but sweet. An opening door, a collapsed surface, no matter how artificial. Does it go on forever, he wonders. Melodrama? And the sudden impulse to phone again. Get himself out of this self-inflicted paradise. Only this time he can't because Sarah and her mother are camping out at Ellison Park.

Where there are no phones.

He'd seen them off early that morning, all three of them
joking about the enormous amount of food and equipment
they were taking for a three-day stay, about all he'd
accomplish now that he had some *freedom*, about how the car
would break down half-way there, or how monsoons would
sweep them back early. All winking and scoffing and chuckling. Surfaces. And at the back of Sarah's mind, as she
squinted at him through the car window in its slow arc out
of the parking stall, a sure knowledge which he'd tried, as
usual, to conceal from her: that he needed, simply, to be alone
for a while. Ironically, she could understand this need and
accept it whereas he had to approach it by as many convo-
luted ruses as he could invent. It was something she was
happy, even relieved to accommodate. Sarah was so honest
about what he needed to make him happy, he so confused.
So, I've packed her off, he thinks, and have this time now.
Have shut in this time for myself. For the visions. And he
glances idly about the kitchen, searching.

At least the stove and the fridge work here, he sighs.
Except for the overhead fan above the stove. When Sarah had
first showed him the apartment he had been ecstatic. She led
him from room to room to show him what she'd done. After
they'd decided to move to Vernon for at least a year, she'd
come ahead from Regina while he'd finished off his teaching
at the university there. She was beaming at him. See? They
now had a wonderfully furnished apartment in Vernon for
the whole summer! And she'd done it all on her own for the
two of them. So their slow waltz through these rooms was a
dance of new things to see and feel, a waltz whirling in
congratulations and glee.

The bedroom was a nice size with a good double bed. It
was off the floor, too, which was a first for them. The bathroom had new fixtures and a shower as well as a tub. The
shower was another first. The livingroom broadloom was
cheap and stained, but it seemed a luxury to have all that
wall-to-wall. Another first. There was even a gigantic sliding

glass door that opened onto the lawn which spread down to the creek. And the stove had an overhead fan for odours. So they put on his favorite Randy Newman album and made love in their new, crisp bed, made love to their new place.

Sarah's happiness in their dance had been so obvious in her blushes and by the way she'd orchestrated their slow turn through it all, surprise after surprise. There had been a joy in it for him, too, certainly. But he knew that he made that so difficult to surface. Moments like these terrified Peter sometimes because he wanted to experience them so much that he watched himself watching himself in them. He felt such a deep, guarded passion for Sarah's joy that he was fearful of these moments, afraid he'd spoil them with his confusion about them. The sides to all these manoeuvres to plumb and sustain their happiness contained his own glee, and he'd grown to believe that this containment was the fullness of it for him, that he would miss out on hers always. He didn't know how or why this happened to him. Even those questions seemed, simply, a natural part of these moments, a part he would try to conceal in his eyes.

And in those other moments, too, when he cradled her head in his flexing hands and entered her so that she began to murmur to him involuntarily, gently at first, then in a distanced fierceness, even then his joy was qualified, guarded by the film he saw of all this. His anxiety intruded, too, to colour the scene in a pale, pastel wash. His fear that he might come too soon; fragments of letters in *Penthouse* or *Playboy*, pieces of film in which Sarah abandoned herself with someone else, these played upon his hesitant joy. They closed in upon him like a habit overtaking him, propelling him to a perspective which he sensed was corrupting him at the same time as it fed him. Gave him purpose: to survive all those letters and movies, those cameras, those limited surfaces: to be, at some price, original.

And it didn't take much time for Peter to realise that their first dance through the apartment had been, in another, delayed way, an artificial surface, an abstraction. He'd expected that. The truths set in like doors closing. These were important doors, too, for he believed in interpreting and plumbing those surfaces, had come to know how *things* worked, were made, how the real textures of the rooms and objects he lived with shaped him. When he moved here to be with Sarah, something in him knew that he was entering a new territory. The motion of his life was slowing down and he had begun to focus on things, to see things more clearly, more intimately. Instead of the distraction of speed, he was being offered a cathedral of stillness, filled with objects. It was a frightening gift to be offered and his instincts were all wrong in the face of it. He didn't know what to do. He didn't want to admit that this new landscape terrified him, overwhelmed him by its lack of motion. He knew on another level that he was being offered what he'd always wanted: the time to see through things. So he did. He did see through things, and what he saw terrified him. And more than at any other time in his life, he understood how distraction is the grease of life. How it feeds a motion that is absolutely essential. Arrested before its objects, the human mind is terrified by their intensity, their falseness, their fragile depths, their beauty. He had entered the garden he'd always avoided, and he was entering it with a skill to see it closely. This was the first stage. Here. These things in front of him, here in this small apartment, would have to be seen through before he could survive this stillness, before he could relax into this garden. It was not going to be easy. He knew that. Even joking about it couldn't alleviate that struggle.

The bed creaked horribly. The gyproc walls were substandard, beneath paper-thin. The sliding glass door had no screen against the thousands of scheming bugs which advanced towards them, clicking their sinister paths across the lawn from their dark homes by the creek. The fan above the stove was cosmetic. It was not vented out; it merely recirculated the smells out over your head into the small, closed kitchen. All of these closing doors seemed insignificant,

however, compared to the slow slam on summer caused by
Carl and Leslie when they moved into the apartment above
Peter and Sarah's. Carl and Leslie began to turn Peter and
Sarah into a parody of the easily disturbed, elderly couple,
pursing a communal mouth in endless disapproval of the
raucous crescendo of destruction gathering above them. Carl
and Leslie began to ruin an idyll of summer like rain. They
forced Peter and Sarah inside, into a seething, fuelling anger.

Carl was an immature nineteen. His chief passions were
his self-immolating 1964 Pontiac, beer, and dated heavy-
metal rock music played at full volume. Because he was
unemployed he had all the time in his world to refine these
passions in his own slovenly, polyphemic way. Leslie was
sixteen, pregnant, and melodramatic. Though Carl tried to
ignore the child growing in her, Leslie couldn't help trading
in futures. She alternated her conduct between one vague
movie of whatever doubtful romance and fun had thrust
them together in the first place, and another screenplay of her
mother's world, a script of conventions and responsibilities.
She'd ascend the outside stairs to their apartment one night
loaded on lemon gin or gleefully paranoid on acid, laughing
and hooting. The next night she'd be shouting at Carl, scold-
ing him for his full, easy ways, shrieking out for order,
stuffed with age like an ancient shrew. Surprisingly, Carl
seemed indifferent to these alternating moods in Leslie, and
indulged himself with astonishing zeal. One of his choice
indulgences was to bring back about twenty sixteen-year-
olds from the public beach late at night and introduce them
to booze, dope and acid.

They'd pass by Peter and Sarah's window, this Bosch
relief of the blind leading the blind. They'd pass as faltering
shadows behind the curtains beneath which Peter and Sarah
lay wide awake, blinking, controlling themselves. These
shades would be lurching, stumbling, barfing, laughing, falling. Inevitably, every second night or so, one of the initiates
would reveal, in some pathetic monologue that made Peter

wince, that this was the first time: "Gawd I'm drunk. . . shit.
. . I'm. . . loaded. . . whew!"

In time Peter—who thought he was so liberated—turned
into some fanatic Ebenezer, and lost control. One night he
planted himself on the asphalt beneath their apartment in his
bare feet and his frenzy, wearing only his jogging shorts and
an old black leather jacket he'd bought years ago in Edmonton after seeing *Easy Rider.* He yelled at the top of his voice:
*"If you fucking assholes don't leave or shut up I'm going to haul in
the cops, right fucking now!"* On another occasion, grown
delirious in a mushrooming, obsessive conspiracy against
Carl and Leslie, Peter pressed his face against the screen to
the bedroom window and began to imitate a rooster while
Sarah laughed, crazy on the bed beneath him. This tactic
climaxed when Leslie, in her fathomless stupor, whispered
dramatically to one of the young guests: "Hey. . . there's a
chicken down there. No. Really. Ssssshhhhh!" Then, after a
pause, "Hey! Who's got a chicken in this place? There's
sposed to be no pets. Hey Carl!. . . Hey!. . . where's *Carl* for
fuck's sake? *Carl!* No. C'mere. There. Listen! There. There's
a goddamn *chicken* down there!" And when Peter gauged
that both Carl and Leslie had wedged their ears as close as
possible to the balcony railing, he clucked three times, then
whispered in a loathsome monotone: *"I* am the fucking
chicken down here, and I'm going to scratch and peck my
way into the kitchen now and phone the cops. Carl, you're
going to get busted for contributing to minors. *Get that, Carl?*
They're going to throw the book at you, you fuckhead, and
you'll do at least twelve months on Okalla. Can you understand that Carl?" Peter unleashed one last triumphantly
rasping crow and slammed the window so hard he unsettled
the frame from its cheap aluminum track. He returned to the
bed where Sarah lay in disbelief, refusing to accept they'd
been shoved this far into cartoon.

You get inured to some things, Peter thinks, tweaking his
nose, eyeing the quiet ceiling cautiously, wondering if Carl

and Leslie had gone out to the beach early, or, more likely, hadn't gotten up yet. He rises out of his chair now, stretches, walks over and turns on the radio on the kitchen counter. He can't even get CBC-AM here because he doesn't have an FM dial. In the Okanagan, and in other valleys in the interior, you either couldn't get CBC at all, or you could pick up the AM on your FM dial. You could only get CBC-FM, however, if you paid for Cable TV and hooked it up to your radio. This bothers Peter because no matter where he's lived these past ten years the CBC has remained a constant, its familiar voices like another volume in his home, a comfort. Shit, he thinks, turning off the local talk-line on which every issue was solved irredeemably, and stands instead in front of the screen he'd built for the sliding glass door.

He'd done it quickly, but fairly well, because of the bugs. He'd bought a roll of fine mesh screen and stretched it onto a grid of door-frame stripping. His screen fit perfectly enough, slid fairly smoothly along its metal track. Late at night sometimes, when he'd sit at the table with his papers glancing up through the screen to the charcoal sounds of the creek, he'd have a vision of the world pressing on its thin surface: thousands of moths pressing up against his wall as if the wire mesh were his own stretched skin, tiny fierce eyes attracted to this light, wanting in. Why am I so uneasy about all those insects out there, he asks himself now. I've screened them away in fear. As he returns to his papers at the table he feels like some failed hermit, a timorous recluse from the elements. Unnatural, he sighs, disappointed with himself again. As if he were failing in some role, the cameras catching him: a pathetic anti-hero trapped with little dignity by his own, self-inflicted insecurities. The kind of character in a movie whom you dismiss in a conversation in a café following the movie, scoffing at the ineffectual role he'd played as the fall guy to the legitimate and interesting dramas of the real hero and heroine — who acted, who made decisions, who satisfied themselves.

Later, Peter looks up from his notes to catch the time on the face of the plastic radio. 2:00 p.m. Shit. The boredom of his task is driving him crazy today. Look at me, he thinks, here I am in my perfect fantasy and I can't stand it, I need something else to happen, some knock at the door, some opening into fun. What is the matter with me? He looks sideways at Lowry's novel.

So what?

The closed world of that man, he thinks, it's a closed world. And I reach tentatively through broken, still shattering windows to touch cold flesh, seek out the life beneath it. But Peter has forgotten how to do that. Originally, he'd been determined to catch Lowry's sense of volume rather than space, open up that man's way of seeing the thickness of things, the volume beneath the surfaces, and the walls we erect around it to protect it. He wanted to illuminate that gift of layered, shifting life that he knew was always there in Lowry, like hearts beating. So he thinks instead of his close friends. Of their hearts. Beating.

You are each closed off from me now, he thinks. You're sitting in other rooms — in Nelson, Edmonton, Lloydminster, Regina, Toronto. What are you thinking about? Where are you when I need you to show up suddenly, today, knock on that door, or better, appear as a smiling vision behind the sliding screen door? Where does this everlasting sense of disappointment come from? Why am I bored by myself? Beside myself with boredom.

He laughs suddenly, humored by the schizophrenic possibilities in that.

Beer would . . . the fridge might . . .

Instead, he considers the world falling outside beyond the screen. The birds are wild today with noise, having fun, being themselves. It's one of those high, arching Okanagan summer days. It's already 33°C out there under that sun. Absolutely exquisite out at the lake where the body dips in and out of the water, diving downward, resurfacing to the gold air again. And later, stretched on a towel, the body preens and tans and sighs. Fun. It's so perfect out there, he thinks, and remembers the summers of his childhood, the scaled-down perfects of the Scona indoor pool where he and Richard would spend the whole day swimming lengths, perfecting dives and cannonballs, returning later into the afternoon sun, weaving down 106th Street exhausted, chlorine-eyed. It's so goddamned perfect here I might as well be cast in some TV commercial, the ideal landscape of summer. I felt that same resistance years ago with Carol when we walked the wide beaches at Cape Cod. Why this resistance, he wonders. I hide like some sleuth who's being paid by an indifferent, cynical god. I sift through the darkness in cafés and bars looking for flaws. Why not simply get out there, get some exercise and a tan, become an Okanagan jock? Jesus. Why am I sitting here like this, asking all these ridiculous questions when I could just go and *do* something? Go to The Coldstream for some draft? Have a few bottles here? That'll perk me up, get me rolling. It's so hot out there. You don't get drunk on four or five beer?

The vein in Peter's temple is throbbing for a beer, for seven beers maybe. He wants to be able to enjoy things, stop these questions, stop the need for answers. How do you get out of this, he wonders.

There's the stained carpet. And there's the tiny late-sixties stereo which Sarah had unearthed in her parents' basement for their albums. Yes. And all of Sarah's plants and pottery. Beautiful. Surely. Indian cotton arranged delicately over all of this, transfiguring the whole into what once had been Peter's late-sixties heart's desire, his dream of the garden: living in some understated, colourful town nestled into the interior mountains, free, writing, loving someone in all this green mountain air. A pastoral. So live in it, you idiot! What is going wrong here?

I know what it is, Peter answers meaninglessly to himself, then forgets.

I don't know much anymore.

He walks to the sliding screen door and all movement becomes slow motion, impressionistic, a perfectly stilled summer camera. He can almost spot the lenses whirring in the bushes as he slides the door backwards and passes through it, laughing with himself, some hero. The camera pans from his bare feet deep in the thick grass to his hand cupping itself over his forehead to shield his eyes as he gauges the sun. Looking over at the tumbling creek now, his sense of humor returns. He sees that other self now, that self behind the screen, sitting at the table, staring back at him with belligerence, and fear. Then it turns to the table again, rooted in restlessness to those books and papers. Ludicrous.

What is it? What is it? Be honest now.

He lies full length under the sun by the creek and stares through his fingers at the sky. Though he shifts nervously at first, eventually he allows the ants and other insects to have their way. He lets his mind become all this green and heat and light. In time three things occur to him almost simultaneously, like gifts: he doesn't have to try so hard; to overcome fear he has to accept the elements; and finally, that he has become an exile — not merely from the elemental world around him but, more important, from his own body. He considers each of these slowly, promises he'll write them down in big letters on a large sheet of paper and force himself to read them each morning in the bathroom.

He stares back at that cynical resistance behind the screen. Still working futilely in that lesser world. Stares at that humbling image fading now into sepia as it rises and lurches toward the fridge. He knows suddenly what's wrong here: since we don't know how to live in nature any longer we build the surfaces of an artificial one which soothes us, but which, essentially, we are unhappy in. So we constantly measure, trim, cut, mow, arrange, transform, anaesthetize everything beyond the screen we see through into some safe, geometrically calculated Eden. And sometimes, when we're bored enough to really look into its surfaces, we admit that they nauseate us, violate some deep instinct, a lust for uncontrolled vegetation and flesh: some violent, chaotic landscape which would occupy us fully, and through which we would move sensually, without fear, no time for it. Ah.

So he scans the deep blue unmapped vault up there. His eye moves cautiously to the image behind the screen, shuffling through a kitchen drawer, and then careens back up to the sky. From the screen to the sun. I don't have to try so hard. I must remember to open myself up and touch things.

As the beer bottle cap clatters into the garbage bag, Peter stands transfixed. He reminds himself — with a grim, determined constriction of his face, in a calculated stare that pivots around his thinly drawn lips as if he were being filmed forever — I must remember to open myself up and touch things.

As in a time warp, the Jefferson Airplane blows the lyrics to *White Rabbit* down through the trembling, fragile ceiling like a primordial wind.

Carl and Leslie are up now, having fun.

two

in the gardens

for the big grey room

ENCLOSED GARDEN, 1

have been tending private gardens instead

pass through the grey film of the door
descend blue stairs armed with clippers
trowels   gloves   pails   rakes   a variety of
sprinklers on hoses   the lawnmower

groom lawns and flower beds
plant annuals   a clematis
a virginia creeper

ceremoniously install a tamarisk
a sun-burst locust

trying to break the linear mathematics
of our standard city lot

and yet simultaneously
I attempt to manicure this garden
into another order

we commit this contradiction on ourselves
not as innocent as instinct versus reason

as if contrary selves
perceived alternate beauties
we are at war
growing ourselves chaotically
rearranging   reordering

this garden

is always two photographs of itself
one superimposed upon another

they never match up

these photos

unless a third synthetic self
leans back into this striped canvas chair
stretches its limbs

at peace in this vortex of wills

watches the water whirl round and round

drenching a porous ground with

possibility

ORIGINAL SINS

So it must have been after the birth of the simple light
in the first, spinning place
—*Dylan Thomas,* Fern Hill

1. out at the cabin   this time
   colour saves me

   home to the still lucid

   agreements   negotiates

   a puzzling

   peace

2. blue and red striped vinyl lawnchairs
   collapse in a broken ring around the peeling
   blistered cedar table

   totems of last night's party

   husks of the assymetry of our apotheoses
   discarded glasses   bottles   cigarette packages
   suggest the fuel of these ascents
   into artificial   only imagined
   innocence

   Eden

   the sun shreds the lip off
   the yawning slumped mountain across the lake

   I blink

   five blue and white oildrums
   glisten at the far end of the dock
   catch the sun randomly
   in their lilts

   it is abrupt:

robins and starlings sweep down from the blue air
like rain   and out of the dark stretched lake
silvered carp and aluminum trout whip up to that air
while the gauze willows round the cabin shudder

this landscape strains
in the white light of itself

unselfconscious leap of life
enfolds me like dream
a world spinning within itself
its elemental song   celebration
in blues

original garden
never evicted from itself

I sit here in the knowledge of this
in the heart of its blue life

Adam: wondering   confused

squinting his eyes into this sun

listening for voices and instructions

preparing apologies

GHOST IN THE VORTEX

1.
it was difficult to see the body at first
concealed between the sumac and the pine
in the soft velvet grass

it hadn't been there
when we left to walk the dog
must have materialised later on
as we chuckled over the asphalt sideroad
clucking to Georgia who was blameless in glee
snuffling in her street world bit by bit
her coat flailing the eyeline a mop against the sun

(you get nervous sometimes
when you see your simple joys filmed into
Dagwood Bumstead somnambulances
by that craftier sullen cynicism alive
under lock and key   healthy at the
swirling core of life's idiocies)

we returned from our walk
buoyant in congratulations:
"Wasn't that great?   Aren't we great?
We're doing such a good job, too!
We've been so reasonable about the renovations.
But creative, too!   We're raising Georgia
in the right way: setting up the walls
she needs.   Gee."

until you break this tide
after you raise the venetian blinds
in the whispering living room:

"There's a body out on the lawn."

yes   there is
perfect   still

I peer through the ancient glass
out at this different world
draw my own conclusions:
a middle-aged native Indian
has passsed out on our lawn

it would be our lawn

"What are you going to do?" you ask
coiling back effortlessly from
your various liberations

 I keep staring
notice that the body doesn't move
not even a slight sign of breathing

I can't be sure

I imagine what will happen
if I wake this apparition:
an hour and a half about the bar
what had happened   who had done what
good buddy! me the easy mark
the perfect audience

passing through the archway into the kitchen
I feel my histories whirling around me
a mammoth shrugging beast matted in
its own liberations

like Cuchulain at the water's edge
something deep in me slaughters these visitations
like waves   fights through a current of
ludicrous guilts   impossibly grapples
for the phone

calls the cops

2.
as the blue and white van lurches away
I watch myself from a great distance

am glad
for that sane exile
the hermit who sifts at the far end of my soul
in the midst of such harrowing
pilgrimages

he is welcome

LAMENT

through the squared window
traffic signs the quiet hours in its ink
signatures   rubber on asphalt   invisible
comings and goings   rustling crescendos
parabolic bands stretching this room's vacuums
like   yes   waves licking in to sand

it is soft in here tonight

I'm staring at that rocker over there
carefully   as if it were a guest
I did invite it in here: fixed it last fall
this old relic from Whitby   Maple   Barrie
somewhere north of Toronto
re-dowelled it   clamped it
resealed it   painted that
cream color on it   webbed
its new seat

nobody is sitting in it

curiously enough

nobody is lying naked on that small bed either
gesturing to me silently   turning her head to the wall
drawing her top leg up to her white stomach   stretching
the lower leg down toward me and that blanket
flashing her dark mystery   yes   glistening there
whispering   "Enter me now   here
don't say anything   love me."
one porcelain hand doesn't cup a breast and
funnel downward   over the line of the back
circling a white downed ass   finding that place
then sliding back to the breast again   whispering

nothing I can hear

the woman who is not there is like the rocker
overworked carefully by me   remolded
viced   stuffed with glue and paint   webbed
in greedy affections

in the quiet hour   somewhere   like those cars
waves are releasing her   loosening her
prying her apart so that she is her chaos again

someone else is rocking in her
begins to dream of structure   symmetry

function

ARTIFICE OF ETERNITY

for Reid M. Clarke

we visit your grave tonight
its freshness heaved between
the weathered cement borders
of other older gravesites
under a pearling sky so pink
we think it is coincidence
something you might have arranged

the quiet of this place is loud
with other quiets   I listen
leave her kneeling above you
walk instead among the pines

they sway and crack to the wind
comfort your daughter   my wife
who sits beside you in the mist
talks in the tongue you shared

you a polyphony of quiet anyway
sitting in the livingroom with your drink
speaking occasionally   listening

old man refined into your forevers
I am reminded of you wherever I look
your many instructions out at the cabin
your thirst for order now diminishing
in your absences

none of the rest of us can keep up
with your quiet meticulous ways
your bewilderment over our times
your obsessions for innocence

I peer from the far corner of the cemetery
see her sitting there accompanying your mysteries
crouched between the cement and granite now
whispering

Yeats wished he might become a golden bird

I want this love that seals your burial:

the refinement of her hand as it brushes
the crumbling granular soil above you

comforts you in this dusk

CHIAROSCURO

for Michael Griffin

sitting in his livingroom with him

a cubist sun lifting the walls around us
brushing the Persian rug into its intricacies
whispering a brightness like a fuse in the air

we talk of darknesses

we were simple men once who loved the air
and all the bright things falling round us in the skies
— a midnight rain which turned the sidewalks into
mirrors   the smell of them soaking into asphalt
a morning moon whisked Japanese by the birches
the mid-day heave of the body in a closed car or
some shattering white walls of David Milne snow —
and any light dreams rushing downward in the skies

that's how you approach these doors:
carrying a bright light with you in your hands

but now we speak of pills and booze or
why we shouldn't speak of them
we think like bats   feeling our way
in charcoal glimpses of our day to day
and fumble with our hands flat on the wall
finger-tipping for cracks to let in light

when our world chose to forget itself
it fell asleep into dreams of walls and floors
in these dreams there is geometry
an architecture which breeds darkness
shuts out light

when the world we made chose this sleep
it dreamed a mathematical image of itself
which holds us   still
and counsels us to fall asleep
so we become part of its machinery

and since our friends chose to live that sleep
we meet secretly in darkened rooms and
open the drapes a bit to remember

we are losing this small purchase
we have on light
while darkness gets as thick as a day

some great hunched creature eats its way
into our eyes so that we barely recognize

the sighs that rob the air

STUDENT RECITAL: HOLY THURSDAY, 1980

(dark

that muscled sky above his last imperfect night
exhausts   sweats   him kneeling in imperfections
pleading the perfect   whence it comes

these agonies of tending gardens in the spring anyway
stepping lightly everywhere with hoses and cans
feet lifting in life: the green shove   erratic
vulnerable   relentlessly pushing yet drawn up
underground plots to get at that sun somehow
be sucked up into it from this thick shaded

dark)

my ear is some Platonic vessel they fill
it knows beforehand what is to come
two sure things: the music they play
and the other music they don't play:
it is perfect and plays along with theirs
overlapping   simultaneous

my ear is a concave spy
erecting walls around their billowing air
guarding for leaks   mistakes   misplaced doors
finding these everywhere

where does this notion of smooth architecture come from?
what draws me   unexplained   into perfects?
causes twitches   abrupt breathing
agonies of the falling short of
agonies of gardens in spring?

why would I want to perfect these anyway?
cultivate their music into some polished form
when I don't listen to my own junk sing
screech its life into wings and debatable air?
satisfied to arch up through this dark and improvise?

I leave finally as some pompous machine
Wyndham Lewis might have drawn
all levers and gears
grotesque spidersteel ear:

thwacking o'er the carpet through the door
propelled by their imperfect grease

and bound
           to keep running
                         perfectly

THE UNNECESSARY TORTURE OF SUMMER NIGHTS

the street is a caragana of quiets tonight
so thick so loud you'd think something in it
would crack and shred these hesitations of
light and wind   these pauses in air

but the street sighs into its own shadows and sleeps
its different dreams

I sit in the outset of these territories
barely breathing on the porch step: a conscious eye
in the heart of this unconsciousness
a scythe through wheat

my dog wedges herself closer to me
for protection

(and we have invented the usual
signs to define ourselves in this
then judge ourselves accordingly
finally despair of the signs
why would we be enclosed by them?

and we have scripted the usual
films of our day to day lives in this
cast ourselves in a variety of roles
then abhor the movie and its heroes
why would we want to watch ourselves
watching ourselves like this?

"It's all in the mind."

that's where it is all right

why would we want to suffer
these distances by such callous
measurements?)

streetlamps pace and orchestrate the dark
trail their auras down the misting street
to the corner where the penny-candy store's
Coca-Cola sign strokes the highway
like something sure

beneath these dark panels
the cracked sidewalks sift off into abstraction
evanesce into charcoal

livingroom windows cast fuses of light
like the glowing tubers of circus tents
over the stretched geography of lawns
while one unattended sprinkler cuts
through the quiet a lion-tamer's whip
whirling circles

my feet fumble unconsciously for leverage
rearrange their gravity on the wooden steps
as my dog attempts even closer contact
nudging her encrusted bum onto my pantleg

over my shoes to the south
the looming black sillouettes of a Maple and Elm
clutch at the sky like flayed roots
the moon a grail in gnarled fingers
those intricate histories

there is nothing to say

I sit in this garden
the air a fuse in my face
the light and heat of summer
abstracted by night

what would I want to say anyway?

(would it be better
if the trucks rolled in
cameras hoisted down onto dollies
the crew instructed
the director poised
in certitudes?

could I film a better version of this?
me the solitary wise vortex of the scene
designed to make the frantic suffer
toss in sleep for parallel perfections
excluded from this one?

isn't it enough?
a man sits before the oncoming summer rain
sifts in these silences
for the silences themselves?

is here in this blast of living
an eye on the imperfections of Eden?

must we always diminish ourselves
package our going in order to see it

disappoint ourselves in mirrors?)

rain descends like rain
drapes this naked world in sighs

I cannot believe
the laughter or fear

rain on cement:

my thirty-sixth year

SQUARED CIRCLE

in the garden is
stillness
dreams of motion and
meditations of flight

toward the garden is
mutability
dreams of stillness and
fantasies of stasis

the garden is an illusion of stillness

toward the garden is an illusion of motion

the garden is the stillness of the soul
by the persistence of the heart

toward the garden is the motion of the heart
by the resistance of the soul

nothing is redeemed

everything is redeemed

IN THE REAR-VIEW MIRROR OF THE FINNING CAT

Under the skin, is a huge rubbish heap of crumbled congealed magma and dead bodies, pressed into stone over countless millions of years.
—*Edward Hyams,* The Changing Face Of Britain

the first bones it unearthed were fresh:
heaved pets   the rattling carriages of birds
traces of human foetus   recent death

you can ignore this close archaeology he thinks
and the weighted cat carves farther into this hill
the underpinning of the old site of Strathcona
his burrowing part of an effort to relieve
a traffic problem: dissecting Edmonton's valley
walls into efficient corridors   knifing deeply
into its exfoliate past

but as the weeks wore on   and he increasingly inward
the low fall sun   the vacuum of the headphones
buried him inside the cab   the only point of contact
that squared castiron jaw extending beneath him
churning up more and more bones farther in

as if it were his jaw

and his eyes bore into the hill in front of him
saw the skeletal death emerge before it was hoisted
clinging   tendrilled history   over his head
sifting down like reasonable patterns into trucks
drawing up behind him to receive this freighted past
saw part of   then the full force of   the Old Vision:

primeval Sponge: ironic inverted Babel
we dance our straining jig upon   our feet kissed
by its growing   decayed suction   smacking
our leaps forever deeper   downward into some thing:

a world of after-images

of the Worm

laughing dancers sway   hoist faces upward
into sun   half men   half meal
only the torsos twisting in the delight of eyes
while the old jaw works away   draws
the tableau down into the calcium ritual:
a last dream of sponges   final ironies   alive
by empty spaces   once the shouting dancers themselves
now a quiet vacuum of this breathing   undulating thing
fed by negatives   in its own dry way   alive

it was shortly after this assignment that he'd go
to the Strathcona Bar too often   sit there
comfortable in the patronising indifference of
his future: lilting in the students' laughter

it was their bar   their dance now

tap his aenemic foot on the sponge of the broadloom
slapping spilt beer to the persistent clumsy jaw of the juke
box

his head an unearthed hill

OUTSIDE THE SYLVIA

for Joan

monolithic logs heave and interrupt the beach
every fifteen seconds a jogger in bright clothes carries
the sand to the sky somewhere nearer Stanley Park
Beach Avenue rattles its supper traffic

gargantuan elms oversee these
their branches scratch at the low soup sky
fracture the soft distances of the bay

farther down the street
next to a flashing red traffic light
are the forest green awnings of an
expensive restaurant

pastel apartments hunch and hover in the wind
crowd the quilted patches of green grass and
the many-colored people switching over them

everything is in motion

the skyline Kitsilano

as I look away
fifty seagulls implode
a collapsing beige umbrella
on a middle-aged woman's hand
flinging birdseed onto the sand

then the seagulls depart

umbrellas unfurl everywhere

all the car lights switch on beneath
the green awning and the traffic light

only the sea is still and even it is

still moving

COLD WAR: REMEMBRANCE DAY, 1983

for my father, Harry

1.

she and her mother are going by bus to Vancouver
I drive them up to Kamloops early in the morning
so they can catch it there and save time

my father is away visiting in Edmonton
I have borrowed his new car to test it out
this 1982 Buick Skylark
the best car he's ever had

the drive up vanishes in company and stories
these ricochet off the new vinyl seats

departures are like this   ignore the world

left behind later
the world replenishes itself in new silences
I thrum my fingers on the steering wheel

my father's presence comes unbidden
unsummoned

it is an odd commingling

the two of us puzzling out this day

(not as Hamlet's father
all rags and steam and fingers wobbling for vengeance)

puzzling out this day

2.

He is one of those men who never talk about the war. Not
outright. All we knew was that he had been a sergeant. My
mother had saved the three stripes and some medals he

didn't care about. He had been a gunner. When I was twenty-
one, I drove up to Grouard to drive him down for the
weekend. We were just about the only thing moving on the
highway that night, the headlights burrowing an endless
charcoal, tunneling south. In that darkness he did ramble on
about the war for no apparent reason. He drove a truck, he
said. One time, when he'd stopped for a coffee and cigarettes
somewhere in Belgium, his jeep was blown up while he was
inside the canteen. Funny stories about arriving back three
days late from a weekend pass in Paris. A young woman he
had gone out with near the training camp in south England.
Suddenly, he was talking about these things. They seemed
to me then, for I was so young and confident, to be the surface
of a dark volume in which my father lived. Just north of the
turnoff to the Alaska Highway, I ran over an animal in the
darkness. "Don't worry about it," he said. "Watch the road."

3.

in the bus depot we talk over coffee
she and I about our new approach to money
her mother gives advice   then her clustered
muscled stories of the war in Ontario
working as a nurse in Kingston
with the wounded

the things she'd seen

stories that chafe the world we'd arrived at
the molded plastic surfaces of the new depot
the motels and modest retail malls around it
the women's auxiliary and its poppies in the lobby
exuberant with the faint air of 1944 canteens
clinging to their starched white blouses

the five or six losers shuffling their feet pointlessly
casualties   pathetic in the plastic slung chairs
glaring sideways at the row of lockers
or more hopefully for obvious suckers like me

they might glean on to pull them through
this holiday

and yet this new world
bouyant in its mindless absence of obvious war
exists in direct contrast to those landscapes
through which the grey men snaked
armed in darknesses
uniformed

this is the world they might have imagined

they were fighting for

it is possible

some young soldier lying on a beach
blinking into fine gravel   convulsed in pain
imagines the world I have my coffee in

me a focused part of
this man's vision

his child of the future
he sees himself

bleeding into

4.

One afternoon after my parents moved here to Vernon, I was
shopping in a bulk-food store, scooping some peanuts from
a bin near the vast plate-glass window at the front of the
store, when my father pulled up in his new car to parallel
park. The bulk-food store is just down from the liquor store
and I guess he was drifting in for some gin. He parked the
car in a series of pre-defeated, anxious and exasperated
moves, aware of the cars lining up behind him, of the
impatient younger people who had grown into the world
around him. I could tell he was jumpy, annoyed. I could see
him swear sarcastically into the rear-view mirror when a
young guy in a baseball hat honked the horn of his four-

wheeler and, later, see him finger the guy out of the open
window, then laugh, in triumph, to himself. The ability of
this small, wiry man to survive these violences with his sense
of humor, survive them in his own nervous and exhausted
way, intrigued me. He brushed stray cigarette ash off his
shirt, checked out his moustache in the rear-view mirror,
then ascended out of the car, plugged the parking meter,
scanned the sky for portents, and after heaving a great sigh,
set off for the front lines.

5.

on the drive back
silence convenes its own meditations
the landscapes outside the car
whisper into these about
nothing in particular

the hoodoos on the north side of the Fraser
might be cliffs over a beach at Dieppe

there is fresh snow on the crests of the hills
birches have been stripped in the wind

a good landscape to remember war in

the highway is the only living thing
ascending through these anaemic walls
and power poles

in the narrow valley at the summit
husks of farms   abandoned

slash burning all around Monte Lake

a war zone

my father's memories sift these silences
seek images to make them material

I let this happen

in the slow bend approaching Westwold
the word made flesh

6.

like driving into the screen of a movie

beside a fallen grey church
—clacking and floundering in its decay
as an ancient crow in its death throes
out on the lawn in the winter—
there is a cemetery

I had marked its emptiness on the drive up

a crowd of people has materialised

it is 11:00 a.m.

standing in uneven rows on the left side
fifty women in variations of black
shifting occasionally   staring down the sky
taking me in suddenly out on the highway
indirectly absorbed   almost there

facing these
separated by a bright band of musicians
thirty Legionaires in full dress
a rigid grey and white quilt
anchoring ritual

behind these the retreating pastorals
of summer: remnants of green grass and trees
lowing of cattle   spotted white farmhouses
tractors mulching in those far distances

I pass through this tableau like a camera or
a wind slipping through its vague stones

every thing is still

I have been deposited in another time
so close in its differences
I check out the rear-view mirror to be sure
and the movie vanishes into that screen

where did these people come from?
Westwold has a population of fifty

how many young men left these crouched mountains
squinting their signatures from the backs of trains
to die in other tongued hills?

impossible

my passage through their old grief
is the future to its past

I think of other wars naturally

casualties in less physical destructions

trying to fit it all together in that way

useless

7.

pull in for a take-out coffee in Falkland
wedge myself cautiously between my car
and a half-ton

the German shepherd is nervous   panicked
its unevenness framed by the shotgun
resting on the gunrack in the rear window

arms in my wars too

increasingly more

and less psychological

8.

in the Coldstream Lounge back in Vernon
I sip on a double rye
watch the memorial service in Kelowna
on the television

it is crowded in here this morning
the liquor store is closed

we sieze our corners in this village green
like peasants in town for the afternoon
exhausted soldiers on r&r

one couple sits together   conspiring
chuckling   counterpointing good chat
with serious glances up at the service
characters in a Sidney James' movie

these two are my father's age
are happy in here on this day
own the corner of the market
of some mystery

something you understand
in your time

my time full of its own soft schrapnel
is irrelevant to their secret

they share some past
that is present

9.

my father leans back into his green patterned chair

beneath him on the fieldstone to his left
are his cigarettes   the portable radio
his half-finished gin

he is glued to Webster ranting on the television
Webster is passionately mad at everything

Dad gets a kick out of this

sometimes he glares out the window
at the pine-grown mountains
ascending in his distances to the snow
the heavy pendulous skies of November

he occupies the corner of some mystery

today   thinking of him
here in this lounge
surrounded by veterans

I wonder

does he see the world he fought for

out there somewhere?

10.

your face is eclipsed by the sun

the rest of your body moves toward me
arrives at the car in a mocking scoff of surprise

to find me here unexpected

this I remember:

your slow approach down the street
feigning surprise to my futures

"Don't worry about it. Watch the road."

there are wars everywhere

I will remember:

*you clutched the gravel
imagined me perfectly*

ENCLOSED GARDEN, 2

you sway above the center of our garden
tower over a row of green peppers
Botticelli's Venus in running shoes and bikini
rising out of rich and crumbling shells

your hat shades the white sun
a network of light and shadow
on your breasts

your fingers play absently with a wad of weeds
cast the green stalks into the wheelbarrow

as it is filled
the garden is emptied
made darker   more moist
for the sun

you shift the wheelbarrow to the next row
then stop to lean over the feeble fence
scratch Georgia's bobbing head

you grin and coo at our enormous dog
while she quivers her thick neck upward
into the soft gardener sun you are to her
lolls her tongue sideways in ecstasy

when you return to the garden
Georgia stretches out full length
deliberate innocence

I am hidden in the garage doorway
in a long sleeve of vertical light
am here to get everything I need
to rebuild the fence when you are finished
so Georgia cannot break into it again

this is the third time I have designed this fence

I cannot move nor stop watching
fixed by the sight of you
dancing before me in greens
in and out of the sun:
my gardener

Georgia hunkers down into the grass now
groans her pleasure to be near you
her eyes orbs of devotion

I have to laugh at myself
skulking in this darkness
gathering tools to
outwit my dog

undone   made clear
by the sight of you

your willow body should be naked
radiant in this green tapestry
your breasts suspended above strawberries
your thighs whisking through onion stalks

you are the goddess of this place
turn in circumferences of greens
life-giver   warm fingers kneading
the soil into miracles for seed

(and when you sway above me
in our garden thick with night breezes
when I raise my hands to touch your breasts
and our bodies feast upon themselves

you draw me out of a darkness
a seed breaking soil to the sun

or roll sideways and collect me down
to the dark earth of your kisses and

we twist in subterranean pools)

you are the gardener and the garden

we hover round your green marble contours
greedy for the sear of your skin and smile

I open the door into sunlight
Georgia bounces forward to assist me
we descend into the garden

my arms full of tools and wood

to enclose you

three:

facing the gardens

FACING THE GARDENS

for Allan Forrie

1.

this table top stretches out away from me on
the usual cheap vinyl checkered table cloth
a simple white-on-beige geometrical design

circles and squares

her blue visor lies at the far end of these

it is midnight

before me are some books   notes
a manuscript   some chips in a bowl
(these are less salty apparently)

my pen is moving

my eyes are smiling behind themselves

to my right through the pine-sheathed windows
the lake abounds

that's the only word that fits:

abounds in its blue lives: dreams incarnate

the geese have hunkered down on the raft
and are shitting their way into morning

the water laps and suckles the shoreline
sometimes it's a series of rushing slaps
if a boat whisks by in this dark
and you wait for the waves   you time them

across the alternately satin lake
the lights of the subdivision that has
claimed the mountain

shine   and   shine

each glance out into these gardens
differs in what it receives

a band of bombed teenagers stumbles
by on the road talking of booze
living their innocence tonight
their thongs slap the asphalt as
they head for the nude beach

cars slip by on the blue road too
making their furtive rounds: sex

she is asleep in the front room
dreaming of light   of sun

I sit here

keep watch

a shift with myself

hold darkness in squared circles
because it suits me

is part of what I have planned
in this wheel of decision tonight

St. Peter of the crossroads
with his bowl of chips

meditating

2.

the soul turns in its gardens for gardens

for so long I simply moved past them
gardens in rear-view mirrors on highways

— an erratic indrawn prairie town
shimmering its greens two miles off the highway
its bleached totems encased in foliage
what you imagine as the simple grace of
hoses and sprinklers   white picket fences
a summer rodeo   young men and women
in gingham and hats and jeans chawing straw
lovers in the long grass by the nuisance grounds

or the mottled green avenues of mountain towns
plump and excessive in their fake Austrian
English or American facades for tourists
bundled into narrow passes or valleys
leaning together for strength
sly buoyant and rough people
easy with their land   its sexuality
easy with themselves —

I moved past them
never understood those gardens
though I dreamed of them

and my garden

what was being grown
was often passed by too

and after all the bullshit
the lies late at night on the couch
when my hand reached out for
another beer or a rye
elated in its own mindless energy
its momentary deceptions and defeats
after all these rituals

the peace of gardens

always put off

delayed by the party

the soul turns in its gardens for gardens

I couldn't accept that Al
straight talk from the end of the line kiddo
St. Peter of the crossroads   peering out
into the traffic

3.

and who cares for these cliches?

I care   in my own way
that one of us gets this down:

we lived that hard
because we wanted a lot
so we lived that hard and moved that fast we
couldn't help losing what we wanted

I don't seek that forfeit anymore

want to face these gardens

accept what I have grown

4.

a loon calls to the geese

the geese get rattled and respond

some poor loser up on the railroad tracks
barfs on his running shoes

probably thought he was having fun

until now

I consider the gardens I have sewn
while the rhythm of his heaves cautions
my long perspective

I wince and smile simultaneously

not easy to do this

5.

she gets up suddenly and invades
the kitchen. a naked woman
tumbling past as in a movie
— if it were a movie I'd be intrigued by
the possibilities of a surprise coupling —
"I'm not asleep yet," she laughs
sleepwalking through her scene

— her breasts small ripe plums for eating
her pubic hair a soft promise of sweet
delivery from this   she an amazon of
tenderness and rich soils   an ivory
garden I choose to ignore —

naturally   I would forego her touch
for a different kind of nakedness now

I envy her as she stumbles by in
her peace with gardens

yet I admit
we each have a way with plants

6.

the oldest metaphor is the garden

how we cultivate
sew   tend   weed
give life to our lives

it is possible to grow the mind however
and let the body waste in a desert

accept the rich tendrils of one garden
sacrifice another

accelerate through the seasons of
one multifoliate soil

while another ground languishes
choked by its own power for life

by moving as fast as I did
I have separated my life in this way
learned how to use booze to connect
these severed soils   to make them
seem blessed and fertile

an illusion of course   I know

but it worked for a very long time:
I would smile and smile and grin
love everything in my life

love everybody

then abruptly it didn't work anymore
and when I faced that illusory magic
admitted its deceptions I turned

sour   cynical

wept

and under the aegis of a new light
became swaddled in cliches:

obsessed suddenly by balance

water   light

earth   fire

gardens

reduced to elemental cartoons

primitive wisdom

7.

on the way back from the can
the linoleum creaks and heaves its age

I pause in front of a mirror
to check out a mystery

I am a living thing
obsessed by its life

I want my smile back

make a face into the mirror
recognise the child laughing

used to believe that wisdom lay at
the far end of some long procession of thought
it took a life and waited like an oasis
some green garden at the end of a fruitful journey
where you discovered the focussed clarity of trees
after years and years of vague sand and seas

what bullshit
to discover how brief this turns out to be
that one small decision   poorly made
creates a life   or causes ten years to
drop away like this smile from my face

that fast: mutability

motion in the garden

I reassume this seat at the table
stretch my palms flat out on the vinyl

stare at this weave of flesh and bone

the mind recognising its home

so simple to have taken so long to see

a car catapults by full of voices:
"Shit. Am I stoned!"

avoiding the garden is easy

8.

it is 3:00 a.m.

the lake shuffles over in its sleep
breathes more quietly
the geese mutter less frequently

there are no boats or cars
but for the odd thread of imsomniacs whirling
up on the highway three miles away
truckers moving on through blue passes
to Calgary

the kitchen is louder now
the fridge has its own noises
grunts and circulates its cold
the clock paces the room
impatiently consistent
the toaster waits for the sun

this machinery   this artifice
so unlike our own

these artificial gardens we are duped by

ourselves

our delight in the assurance of

machines

9.

how can you love another's body
after having abandoned your own?

I consider my history of sex

imagine highways   machines
freeways   speed   motion

illusions of journeys

restless mechanical pilgrimages

drawn on by the white steel cathedrals
of pleasure: false bodies   false ecstasies
in false aluminum photographs   soft movies

the advertisements for Eden that enslave us

our pampered grunting races
for the quick fix

momentary highs

and yet I have loved flesh
have lulled this motion into pools of eyes
have been arrested by this sleeping woman
in that farther room

and others

have been stalled into joy

what is it that is bothering me?

what is it now?

10.

only my innocence
would even bother to wonder at all this
otherwise I could simply fuck my way through
these gardens   until at last exhausted
in some epiphany over a bedpan
I might suddenly see the procession of my life
and arch back into the headboard   killed by
the shock of the pleasure I avoided for

motion

only my innocence
attempts to salvage anything in this

11.

and the booze

holds the illusion together
insists that these artificial gardens are real
while miles away
in some dark thicket of birch trees
a real garden waits
or just our own bodies wait
surrounding these alternate ecstasies
like a landscape not seen

or even the real flawed gardens
we have grown wait

to be seen or

named

12.

and the excuses we fashion
for these thrilling journeys away
from the body

Rimbaud had some good ones

or fame and fortune are good ones

so-and-so's ascendancy
what's-his-name's fall
those capricious hierarchies
that make fools of us all

these things are smaller
than we are

more false
nothing to be listened to

though we bitch and whine we
are blessed by voices around us

who cares really if we rise and fall
as long as we say something about it:
what it was like to turn in
these jewelled mixed territories
be alive at all

13.

I wanted so much to see you again
and when you came I drank your visit away

who can explain such contradictions

such panic in the heart?

and all that false emotion that
insists itself into the spaces of affection
when you get bombed?

what could I say afterward?

we are old drinkers you and I
know enough of those gardens
to forgive them their sins

that's not good enough for me now

that dance misrepresents my light
exchanges it for a pathetic darkness
melodramatic   insistent
boisterous   defiant

a self unlike this quiet man
who sits here now remembering highways

recalling distances

so I gulped down several C-2's in the morning
as the mindlessly optimistic furnace man
rushed round the house cleaning air ducts
of dust and dirt and foul air

I sat holding my head in my hands

I almost thought that he'd been sent to claim me

14.

this night out here has reached
its slowest vigil

and no birds sang

the shore and the water have concluded negotiations

it is so quiet I can hear
the streetlamp up on the road

even the fridge has conceded

I begin to settle too:

face my gardens
my litanies of light and growth
my matins for a soul:

> I have lived swiftly and smiled much
> I have had great pleasure in my time
>
> *O Lady of the velvet highways*
> *unroll my soul*
>
> I have always remained innocent enough
> to be surprised   delighted   angered
> and to recognise the good in that
>
> as I sit here
> in this small pine cabin
> on the lip of this soft white lake
> I draw my past within me
> recognise its bounty and its weeds
> know that it will always be this mixture
>
> *O Lady of the table top*
> *bless these contradictions*
>
> I have given to other people
> I have given to myself

I have indulged others
I have indulged myself

I have worked hard
I have been unconscionably lazy

O Lady of the terry-towel bar table
forgive these indiscretions

I have been achingly sober
and blisteringly drunk

I have made choices
choices have been made for me

I have cared for myself
I have ignored my life

O Lady of cliches
grant me their truths

I do not know what to say
I have everything to say about that

I drink too much
I have to stop

O Lady of the vineyards
throw me out

O Lady of the gardens
accept this plant

15.

the charcoal windows shred

above the streetlamps and yardlights across the lake
a mountain emerges and its soft
tumbling edges disclose a sky

this orb of light transforms the world
and the dances begin

the trees come alive with wind and birds
the water reassumes its mouths
the odd car stirs by on the road
as each noise coalesces into light

gold rims the mountains
the sun stretches itself up into a ball
and beams on these triumphs
and a whole thick garden
— bigger than me —
unfolds itself around me
includes me

my heart is like this sun
as it opens on its worlds:

— my brother-in-law Don is somewhere
outside of Winnipeg on a Greyhound Bus
he's in his second day on his way to Ontario
to find a job

        he sees this sun
bless a Wendy's and an Arby's off the highway
notices early coffee drinkers
stepping out of half-tons before work
the bright gestures of people starting
out on their ordinary days

you are somewhere in your kitchen
see this light through your blue Ikea curtains
as the water boils you turn eggs in a pan
call Lynn to tell her breakfast's on

Glen lurches over in his bed in Vancouver
punches the alarm and flicks on the radio
gets his fix of the CBC in this soft dawn

my sister lets the cat out in Edmonton
brings in the newspaper in her mauve housecoat
regards the petunias in that cedar planter
squints at the sky and gauges the impending heat

my mother puts down a pot of tea
wrestles the garbage into a white plastic bag
listens as my father flicks from channel to channel
to arrive at his favorite morning news
these two especially aware of this summer sun
as it sweeps the orange broadloom rug they move upon
fourteen floors now above their old neighborhood
they have ascended to farther views of
their old Edmonton garden: that stucco house
and its back yard full of goodbyes

begin to wonder more about their children's
lives   phone calls   surprises—

this sun seizes each of us in its full force
twists into our tentative stalks and propels us
upward into its faces

we revolve in a muscled elemental grace
of light and dark   unreconciled
turn in blessed and ruined gardens

each of us is a metamorphosis of
bursting green things that fade

we move

then we are stilled

we recognise these things

and do what we can

Epilogue: Mutability

Just a second.

I'll just have another small blast, then I'll tell you what I know or what I think I know about this act here, this art of the middle ground.

There.

Art includes you. It does not kick you out. It will have depths, a slowness of release sometimes, allusiveness, demands to return, subtleties. It has to have these things because we have these things, and it is our music. It is how we think when we try to talk to one another, or when we sit and puzzle the darkness and wonder at the way our lives play themselves out before us. It regrows our gardens, however healthy they might be. And then, over and over again, we rediscover ourselves: we clamber up dark and grey stairs; we brush through cracked and mended doors; we find ourselves running full tilt into whatever these gardens might hold for us. And turn in their bright and green and ambiguous life.

1.

In the morning, as he was washing up the night's dishes in the pine kitchen at the cabin, he listened to CBC's "Sunday Morning" whispering in the background. Occasionally, he glanced sideways out the window to gauge the damage deposited by the geese on the raft through the night. Someone announced suddenly — as if it were common knowledge — that Alden Nowlan had died earlier in the week. Peter stood silent for a moment, his hands unmoving in the suds, his eyes hypnotized by three fall flies lumbering lethargically against the screen. It might have been in the newspapers, he reasoned. He had been avoiding them purposefully since he'd moved out here on his own.

He left a few cups in the sink, dried his hands on the cloth by the stove, and walked over to the door. He stared out at the lake. The water was cellophane-still, barely shifting beneath the low, shredding fog cover that had rolled in during the night from the south, around Rattlesnake Point, and from the east, through the Coldstream Valley. The almost ghastly reds of the trees — especially the violent burgundy of the sumacs along the lip of the shore across the lake — clung to the fog in places, mute, disembodied. And the flat brown pier pushed itself out into this stillness so stealthily that you couldn't be sure where it ended in the thick mist that curled around it. As Peter opened the door and walked across the leaves to the end of the pier, the sharp, unexpected noises he made were violations of these silences. He squatted on his haunches, leaning his elbows down on the denim of his knees, and stared out into it, lighting a cigarette, thinking of Nowlan. Audience monologues. They were in his blood, too. He couldn't shake them.

When he thought of his family he had to laugh for he realised all the self-perpetuating traps waiting for him there, traps he couldn't resist. They had always directed him in some ways, had whispered to him in his vacuums, had mocked him, too, inevitably claiming him. As Del Jordan's magnificently malicious aunts declare in *Lives of Girls and Women*, "pretensions were everywhere." Peter saw — especially in Nowlan's wake — his own father's family: that sarcastic, boisterous, affectionate, indirect and self-celebratory line of Nova Scotian brooders. Their inheritance was a gift and "a pain in the arse" as they themselves might say. Though this inheritance loathed pretensions of any kind, mocking them furtively whenever it saw them, beneath that loathing was an almost diabolical thirst for that same kind of attention for itself: a powerful ego nestling back into itself waiting for phone calls. And beneath that was an even more complex love for almost anything that moved — a love expressed indirectly, of course, in sentimental outburts or maudlin confessions brought on by the booze. Always the booze. Peter saw himself at the heart of these contradictions trying to control them, and he saw that his own heart was buried in that audience, that his voice was trying to free it into some kind of street music. He would use his ridiculous life to sing that audience. He understood that, but he felt, too, as he flicked the cigarette butt out into the fog, that it wasn't going to be easy now. He'd almost given it all away. And he thought of Nowlan again. Peter knew that if he wanted to get it back he was going to have to be stronger than he'd been so far. He was going to have to see something he hadn't seen yet. It was not going to be easy and he wondered — while an even more objective part of him that sat back and watched him squatting there wondered even more — whether he could do it at all.

He stared out into the motionless grey and considered the flashing red life that wove itself into it and surprised it and cradled the fog over the water: this red motion as constant as the fixed chords of the fog were still. In the background he had been aware of the approach of a car up on the highway. Suddenly, he recognised the slow draw of wheels off the asphalt and up onto the fine gravel at the side of the road. He heard a door open and slam. Someone was here to see him. His heart accelerated. He stood and stared up the path to see if he could see who it was. Maybe not, he warned himself. He moved tentatively across the thick red leaves and up the shaded path to find out.

2.

Is it you, then?

July 1984 - August 1989. Kalamalka Lake, Vernon.